# It Starts and E̶

Create your development plan, no one else *should*.

The Nine Steps of Creating Your

# EXECUTABLE

Individual Development Plan

SECOND EDITION

By
**Jasmin NUHIC**

**This, second edition, book has the same goals and objectives, as well as the target audience:**

For anyone that wants to develop and grow more, wants to achieve more, yet needs a plan for how to do it.

For us that strive to reach our full potential and achieve our career objectives, yet do not know how.

# Table of Contents

Jasmin NUHIC

# Preface

I t took six years to write the original book and another two years to publish this, second, edition.
It all started with a personal reflection on my professional development and evolution that I went through. Like many others, I too struggled with my professional development. Without a plan, I was relying on my manager to create one for me. It did not help that I also kept changing my career goals and objectives as well as struggled with the balance between my professional career on one end, and personal values on the other. Then, after more than two years in constant search for the answer, many conversations with senior professionals, as well as number of books read, I realized that I needed to create my own *executable* Individual Development Plan (IDP). I created a roadmap—a flowchart, which became my guide and, later, a guide for many others, towards creation and execution of an executable IDP.

A little over six years ago, I decided to share the same roadmap, the same flowchart, and the same steps with you and others that now read this book. Yes, it took six years because I kept relocating (either for expatriate assignments or full-times roles) to different countries and continents and working for different organizations. These organizations were different in size, work environment, number of people, products they made, and geographies they served. What was not different was my way of creating and executing an executable IDP. I used the same process, the same steps, wherever I was, and with all of my direct reports, peers, as well as professionals superior to me. By doing this, I not only proved that the process works, but also helped many individual contributors, project managers, and people leaders to advance towards reaching their full potential and achieving their career objectives.

**This, nine-step process, of creating an executable IDP can help you reach your full potential and achieve your career objectives.**

What kept me motivated and focused throughout all this time are people like Victor, Kathy, Kevin, C-Jay, Monique, Phillip, and others (I will introduce them and share their stories throughout the book) who struggled as I did. Helping them was my fuel and confirmation that this process works. They all thought they could do more, wanted to achieve more, but did not have a plan on how to do it. Listening to their struggles and helping them overcome them is what kept me going. It kept me writing and hoping that one day there would be professionals like you all around the world following these simple steps and reaching their full potentials and their career objectives.

As you read this book, I suggest having a pencil always handy to take notes, write your thoughts, fill in the margins, and explicitly reflect on your career. In addition, this book should be read with the end in mind. Meaning, this book is written in a way that begins with the end—the result, which is your executable IDP, followed by a number of tips, suggestions, ideas, and examples on how to create it. In this way, you will ensure that you receive full benefit from reading it and use it to create your customized executable IDP. Only by having your executable IDP in place will you work towards achieving your career objectives and ultimately reaching your full potential. Lastly, I suggest getting a copy of this book for your manager as it will ensure that you two have the same point of reference, same expectations, and form true partnership in this journey of yours. Sorry that I kept you waiting....

Jasmin NUHIC
International Author, Speaker, and Coach

# Introduction

D id you know that 97% of the working people work for the remaining 3% of the people? One of the fundamental differences between those two groups of people is that the people in 3% group always had a plan and direction (aka executable IDP) while those in the 97% group did not.

Let me share with you two of my favorite quotes when it comes to the thinking about your career—your executable IDP. First one comes from Abraham Lincoln, the sixteenth President of the United States of America, which says, *"The best way to predict [your] future is to create it."* The second one comes from Peter F. Drucker, one of the well-known and highly respected authors and management consultants, who said, *"We cannot predict the future, but we can invent it."*

I find myself keep coming back to these quotes each time when my career goes awry, and I ask myself a question: "How did this happen to me?" To prevent things from "happening *to* me," I decided that I wanted to predict and invent things that would happen to me—so, I created my own executable IDP.

Furthermore, let me touch on a somewhat relevant topic, a topic that could potentially lead to further research and change of the law. It is related to Equal Employment Opportunity Commission or EEOC. EEOC, according to the official communication, is responsible for enforcing federal laws that make it illegal to discriminate against a job applicant or an employee because of the person's race, color, religion, pregnancy, gender identity, sexual orientation, national origin, age, disability, and/or genetic information. The law applies to all types of work situations including hiring, firing, promotions, harassment, training, wages, and benefits. Consequently, it guarantees employment, or at least fair chance of employment. Yet, EEOC does not include rights (or prevent discrimination) for professional development opportunities. Given the constant changes in labor needs and employment opportunities as well as skills, education, and experience requirements, you can easily argue that creation and execution of an executable IDP should be part of these laws and governed by the EEOC. At this time, this is just a wish on my part, and as I said, a potential research topic (and change of the law) in the future.

Primarily, you should read this book to learn how to create your executable IDP, and then to, in a predictable manner, execute your plan in order to reach your full potential, and achieve your career objectives. My hope is that you will take your learnings even further and help your peers, subordinates, mentees, family members, and friends, with creation and execution of their own executable IDPs—so that they also can reach their full potential and achieve their career objectives. In another word, my hope is that you will "pay it forward."

With that said, amongst many benefits that you should harvest by reading this book, and during the execution of your executable IDP, is that you will end up with a strong network of professionals and friends who will become your coaches, mentors, members of your personal board of directors and, many cases, closer and better friends. Some of the other benefits include getting to know yourself better through personality assessments and self-reflections, and learning your strengths, but also building your network, and being crystal clear about your career path. You will also benefit from learning how to answer some of the most difficult interview questions, such as "Where do you see yourself in five years?" or "What are your strengths? Weaknesses?" or as simple as "Tell us about yourself." I strongly encourage you to identify these benefits as you read this book and start taking advantage of them immediately.

To be able to accomplish all this, keep in mind things I mentioned at the beginning, which is that the best way to predict the future is to create it as well as that you want to be in the 3% group, and not in the 97% group.

Now, this process is not quick (a single event), nor is this process your manager's responsibility, yet it is rather a process, and it is your responsibility. As you read throughout this book, you will notice that each step takes time to complete. There are reasons for that being the case, and you will be able to recognize and understand these reasons when you get to them. Total time required to create an effective executable IDP is fully dependent on your commitment, having a mentor and network, and opportunities within your manager and mentor's circle of influence.

For now, it is also important to, head-on, address your expectations. If your expectations are that it is your manager's job to develop you or promote you into a next level, or if you want to quickly come up with an IDP, or even that you must stay with the same company to be able to successfully execute your executable IDP and reach your full potential, then your expectations need adjustment—prompt adjustment, that is. Your executable IDP, once fully created, is going to be title independent, company independent, and time independent.

In the following sections and steps, I will explain what I mean by "title independent, company independent and time independent," and why setting the right expectations about each of these is imperative for a successful creation and execution of your executable IDP.

This book, and the process described in it, is applicable to all cultures and backgrounds, to left-brainers and right-brainers, to all kinds of careers, organizations, and industries, as well as all levels of any organization. The principle behind the process is based on late Stephen R. Covey's habit two[1], *"Begin with the end in mind."* In short, this book consists of three sections, nine steps, and numerous tools, references, tips, suggestions, and suitable stories which make this book beneficial to you as well as easy to read and follow.

In Section I, you will get introduced to the problem of not having an executable IDP in place, and reasons behind it. This section ends on a positive note as it describes further how you can benefit from this book and solve your problem of not having an executable IDP.

Section II describes and depicts the process of creating and executing your executable IDP. Then, subsequently, helps you learn how to complete each of the steps from a tasks, actions, and results standpoint. Furthermore, in this section, we introduce and explain each of the templates

---

[1] "Seven Habits of Highly Successful People," by Stephen R. Covey

4

that can help you create your executable IDP. Section II is the place where you do the work, and this book guides you to success.

In the Section III, you will learn how to go about executing your executable IDP. You will learn how to maintain and adjust your executable IDP, and how to stick with it when it gets tough. In this section, you can also read about other peoples' success stories. Section III is packed with energy, which is just what you need in order to successfully execute your executable IDP.

Following the three sections, at the end of the book, you will find tools, references, further research and reading, as well as opportunity for feedback that can further assist, and help you on your journey towards reaching your full potential and achieving your career objectives.

Now, sit, relax, and keep reading while respecting and enjoying the process. Let's start, together, the journey of discovering your career path by completing the research and necessary analysis, creating your executable IDP, and working towards reaching your full potential and desired career objectives. And always remember, "It Starts and Ends with an executable IDP: Create your development plan, no one else *should!*"

# SECTION I

## The Problem: Lack of *Executable* IDPs

# Why Don't You Have an Executable IDP?

L et me start by apologizing to those of you who indeed have an IDP in place and have been executing that IDP to better yourselves and the organizations you serve. Furthermore, I would like to recognize you if your IDP is done well and you are reading this book to learn how to improve it. Unfortunately, people like you are rare. Most professionals today, regardless of their level in the organization they serve, the type of organization they work for, or the business or industry they work in, don't have an IDP, much less an executable IDP. The real question, then, is why. Here are a few reasons I've found through interviews and research as well as observation and personal experience since 2002.

## Reason # 1: Lack of Know-How

As you can see in the chart below, the number one reason is that most professionals, whether they are subject matter experts or people leaders, simply have no knowledge of how to go about creating an executable IDP. This should be no surprise, since the process of creating an executable IDP is not being taught in schools and most companies lack a training program, or if they have one, it's poor and ineffective. If you don't possess this knowhow, that's okay, but it is your responsibility to learn. Not knowing how to create and execute an IDP may be acceptable today, but it may not be acceptable tomorrow.

## Why do you not have an executable IDP?

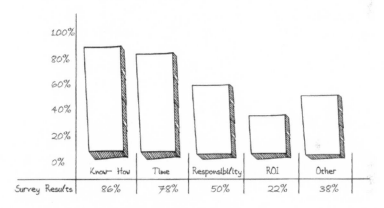

Figure 1: Research results

Victor was a medical device engineer with over twenty-five years of experience, the majority of which he spent with his most recent employer. Victor was happily married with two young sons. In private life, he was quiet and somewhat reserved, while professionally he was very proud of his work, his achievements, and his contributions towards innovations in medical technology. Victor was a solid—not great yet not poor—performer, who strived to become "the best" subject matter expert in his domain. Over time, he subscribed to several professional magazines, attended a number of conferences and countless trainings costing him and the company thousands of dollars and lost opportunities, yet he remained only a solid engineer. What Victor, and the company, failed to realize is that Victor was working from, initially, no IDP and, later, from a very poor IDP. When it came to tough times and the company had to reduce the workforce, Victor was one of the engineers that was let go. Despite all the training and hard work, he failed to reach his full potential, and, with that, position himself as a high contributor. Reflecting back, Victor said, "I never had a chance because I hadn't been trained on how to create and execute an executable IDP." You need to act now, learn and execute the process of creation and execution of your executable IDP to potentially prevent the same faith in your future.

## Reason # 2: Lack of Time

The second reason why most professionals, perhaps including you, do not have an executable IDP, is because of the pressure of "here and now." "Here and now" is the world we live in, the world that is known as "normal" by the millennials. It represents expectation that everything should happen immediately, from work and business results to personal rewards, development, and promotions. Add to those expectations the pressures coming from external factors (i.e. employers) and, all of a sudden, you start to see a big disconnect. From the *external* factors, because of the focus on short-term results, employers have been squeezing every moment of time from their employees. This is a fact. To a degree, it is a goal. In turn, this creates limited to no opportunities to work on creating and executing your executable IDP, ultimately resulting in an entire culture of professionals without executable IDPs. Most notable types of companies that do this are startups, major grocery store chains, and service-based businesses as well as number of large publicly traded companies. But not all are like that. Companies such as Google, 3M, and Hewlett-Packard, Blue Sky, Yahoo!, Condé Nast, Thomas Keller Restaurant Group, National Public Radio, Flickr, and the Huffington Post, as well as number of others, would give you a "free" percentage of work time to work on your "pet-projects." They will also give you "flexible" time that you can spend working on your development. Now, do not take me wrong, the time that these companies are giving to their employees is significant and important, not to say costly, yet it comes in very handy during the execution of an executable IDP. However, just by giving free or flexible time to work on your development, they expect you to know how to go about creating your plan and ultimately creating the right opportunities to execute that plan. In contrast, when you have created an executable IDP, and then been given time to work on and execute it, that is when you and the company benefit the most. That is the sweet spot that makes you more energized, more engaged, and ultimately helps you make a step or two towards reaching your full potential.

From the *internal* factors' standpoint, the personal expectations seem to be that the development shall be an event, an immediate event. This is an unreasonable expectation as creating an effective executable IDP takes time and effort. Between the two factors, external and internal, the internal factor is the one harder to accept by most professionals. The good news is that both can be overcome. This was exactly the case during one of my previous people leadership roles where I managed a team of highly talented, highly educated, and very bright professionals. Soon after taking over the team, I noticed that the gap between the team potential and the team performance results was very large and obvious. It took a solid three months to learn more about the business and the expectations of the business, before I could teach them the process described in this book as "It Starts and Ends with IDP: Create your development plan, no one else *should!*" and then gave them the time to work on executing their executable IDPs. Some of the team members jumped on the opportunity and very quickly made a head start, while others were slower in the process. Eventually the entire team was on board and taking the creation and execution of their executable IDP as serious as the business objectives. The result: the gaps started to narrow, yet more importantly, engagement reached one of the highest (second highest to be exact) in the organization, performance was increasing, the results were better than ever, and ultimately the number of promotions happened. Two team members developed beyond the needs of the organization (outgrew the business) and decided to move onto new opportunities where they were hired at more senior level with increased responsibilities, higher pay, and direct reports. This is what an executable IDP, and the process described in this book, can do for you. Nevertheless, the reason of "here-and-now" is still very dominant, as companies do not allocate time for professionals to work on their executable IDPs, and professionals are not patiently investing their time to create an executable IDP. Which brings me to the next reason, why many professionals today do not have an executable IDP in place, which is "Whose job is it?"

**Reason # 3: Lack of Responsibility**

Lack of clarity about "whose job is it?" is the next most common reason why professionals do not have an executable IDP. So, the question is: Do you know whose job is it to develop you? Or better said: Who is responsible for your development? If you do not know, do not worry, as there are over 50% of other professionals just like you. Also, if you think that having IDP is the responsibility of your manager, then you are 100% wrong. On the other hand, if you think that creation and execution of your executable IDP is your responsibility—your job—then you will be 100% correct. Furthermore, you will also belong to a very small, elite group of professionals that think correctly, and have correct expectations when it comes to development—and being in charge and responsible for reaching your potential and achieving your career objectives. With that said, you are not alone. As you will see later in the book, you have many partners, including, but not limited to your manager, with whom you should work. These partners are essential in developing the best possible executable IDP, and for helping you execute the same IDP. Nevertheless, the ultimate responsibility rests with you, and understanding and accepting that is of utmost importance.

To demonstrate this point, let me introduce Kathy, a colleague, and a good friend of mine. Kathy is a professional in her forties and, as of our meeting time, holds a position of a Project Manager with a global company that sells commodity products in over a hundred and twenty countries around the world. She has been with the same company for close to twenty years. Kathy started as an administrative assistant. Very quickly after, she was recognized for her multi-tasking skills as well as her ability to balance between tasks on hand and people relationships. As time went on, she took on new responsibilities, coordinating projects, and even participating on the projects as a project team member. A few years after starting with the company, she was asked to take a lead on one small local project, which she managed very successfully all the way through to completion. This opened the door for her to move into a Project Manager role, which she gladly accepted. Since then, now over ten years, she has been in this role working on very challenging projects, delivering successful results, and even extending her expertise to other departments— some of which are global. A little over a year ago, she came to visit me and, visibly frustrated, told me how yet again she has been passed over for a promotion. After I offered her a drink, green tea, I asked her to tell me more. This is when she told me all about her experiences, projects, and great work she had been doing. "I missed so much from a personal standpoint—practices and games of my children. I had to travel during birthdays and anniversaries. On the other side of things, I've received many awards, the most notable of which was 'Excellence in Project Management.'" But then, when I asked if the next level, this promotion, was part of her executable IDP, and part of her future, she told me that she did not have an IDP. What is more interesting, she proceeded to tell me that the IDP and ultimately her future, was her manager's responsibility.

At that moment, I asked her to take a big sip of the green tea and reflect on what she just told me. She did so. And she told me again, that in her mind, the responsibility for her development and her future rested in her manager's hands and it has been like that ever since she joined the workforce. Then, I took a big sip of my tea and proceeded to introduce her to the successful creation and execution of an executable IDP—the same material included in this book. For next two-plus hours, she listened attentively and took many notes. She also asked a few questions and, at times, gave me a puzzled look. By the time I was finished, the tea was cold, she was in her deep thought, and I was out of my voice. We looked at each other, acknowledging that this was a long meeting and information-overload.

With that, we parted ways. Fast-forward a few meetings, between Kathy and I, and she realized "whose job is it?" to develop her executable IDP—it is hers!

## Reason # 4: Lack of (defined) ROI

Last but not the least, the reason why professionals, perhaps including you, do not have an executable IDP is because of a lack of clear understanding of return on investment (ROI). Initially, this reason was a surprise to us, especially since we all know that "our employees are our greatest assets," yet the research shows that the development of the "greatest assets" is not being done. Later, through additional brainstorming and interviewing, it became apparent that lack of measurement of training effectiveness is very common across all industries, positions, types of training, and employee development programs. Because of this, I have decided to differentiate between individual training from individual development. This is important, for number of reasons, including but not limited to that training is associated with a job, while development is associated with a career. Also, training is company-mandated while development is individually driven. Finally, in most cases, training is required while development is optional. Once I have made this clear distinction between training and development, it is then when I realize that more work is required in this field—primarily, more research is needed in order to document true ROI due to training and development. Some of the elements that play into this are employee morale, engagement, retention, but also timely completion of work, cost control and reduction, as well as continuous improvement across the entire business.

Even though there is much unknown, the following conversation best summarized this point:
*"CFO: What happens if we train them [employees] and they leave?*
*CEO: What happens if we don't and they [employees] stay?"*

# Why You Must Have an Executable IDP?

E qual Employment Opportunity law may help you get hired, yet no law can keep you employed or prevent you from being laid off, fired, or simply falling behind in your professional development. Only you can prevent that from happening by having, and executing, an executable individual development plan (IDP)—one that takes into consideration the professional, personal, and social aspects of your life.

In the previous chapter, I covered the reasons why most professionals still do not have an executable IDP. In this chapter, I explain why having an executable IDP is a must. Before getting into details and examples, let me ask you this: Do you feel you are in control of your career? Even better, ask yourself the following three questions: Am I growing into my full potential? Am I positively progressing toward achieving my career objectives? Or am I failing to develop and make progress against my personal and professional goals and objectives? Like most other professionals in the United States and abroad, your answers to the questions were probably "no," "somewhat," or "sometimes." These answers, or others similar to them, are reason enough to have an executable IDP.

Wise people, including American football coach Vince Lombardi and former Prime Minister of the United Kingdom Margaret Thatcher, would say, that to increase your chance of predictable success, you should "plan your work and work your plan." Without a plan, how do you know what to work on, and how do you know that your work is taking you toward your desired outcome? Simply put, you do not. Having an executable IDP is a must, for that is what provides the direction you need.

Consider the use of an IDP from a project management perspective whereby you approach career objectives as project objectives. Before you start executing on your project, you get a team involved and create an executable project plan. Understanding that the plan may need to be adjusted and corrected along the way, you start with a plan nonetheless—a plan you and your team believe will lead you to successfully reaching your project objective. The same principle applies here, and this book helps you create your own executable IDP so that you can reach your full potential and achieve your career objectives.

Now consider another general, yet important, perspective. Keeping today's economy in mind, if you are not in the business of learning and developing yourself, you are in the business of falling behind and becoming "obsolete." We must all acknowledge this ruthless truth. We know that a professional recognized as a subject matter expert who does not continuously develop, falls behind professionally and eventually becomes obsolete, outdated. In fact, obsolescence can occur in four years or less. This is a scary statistic, and it is even scarier in industries such as software development and electronics where professionals have been shown to start falling behind as early as every two years.

Obsolescence occurs a) unless you change jobs frequently (which can lead to a negative perception of job-hopping), b) you have progressively increased responsibilities and authorities (job enlargements or job enrichments), or c) you have invested time and money into continuous education with the conscious intention of learning and development. Even continuous education can be problematic. How would you know what to study? What education to get? What skills to develop? What experiences to seek out? Without having first created an executable IDP, decisions regarding continuous education can be hit or miss.

As you read the process described in this book, you will learn exactly which skills, education, and experiences to develop to remain at the forefront professionally and also ahead of your peers. Most importantly, you will be aligned with the industry and ahead of the competition. You prevent yourself from becoming obsolete and may just become an in-demand go-to person. An executable IDP helps you do all that.

The following quote from an unknown origin further demonstrates why you must have an executable IDP, *"A bird sitting on a tree is never afraid of the branch breaking, because her trust is not on the branch but on its own wings."* Two meanings can be derived from it. One being that no matter what your position is, or where in your career you may be, you should never rely on your current state and surroundings. Instead, you should rely on yourself, your skills, education, and experiences. Only your current levels of the same can keep you safe and give you a chance to move if the ground under you becomes shaky. The other meaning is that you should have something that can take you from where you are now to where you want to go. In the case of a bird, it is the wings.

In your case, you must have a plan, and not just any plan, but an executable IDP. This plan gives you your wings (not related to "Red Bull").

Now that you know many, yet certainly not all, reasons why you must have an executable IDP in place, you basically have three options: do nothing different, act and react on ad-hoc basis, or use a proven method to create your own executable IDP, which would help you reach your full potential and achieve your career objectives.

X Do nothing different ⟹ ✗ Act and react on ad-hoc basis ⟹ ✓ Use a proven method to create your eIDP

If you choose to do nothing different, you risk falling behind on your performances, never receiving that promotion you always wanted, and all the while watching your peers marching towards their full potential and achieving their career objectives.

If you choose to act and react on an ad-hoc basis, you risk hitting and missing on two key elements: right time (timing) and right tasks. The ad-hoc option maybe better than doing nothing different, yet it is still far from being sufficient. Yet, if you choose a proven method, systematic method, this method, of creating your executable IDP, then you picked the best option with highest probability of reaching your full potential and achieving your career objective.

In the next chapter, you will learn why this book is good news and a good choice for you, and how it will help you with your career in both short term and long term.

# Why reading this book can help you?

Why should you read this book? What benefit will you receive from reading it? What should you keep in mind while reading it? To answer those questions, let me remind you of a quote you've either heard or read from the late Stephen R. Covey, *"If the ladder is not leaning against the right wall, every step we take just gets us to the wrong place faster."* There's a similar statement that says, *"Some people keep climbing a ladder just to find out at the end that they climbed the wrong ladder."*

This book can help you prevent such things from happening to you AND help you make sure you climb the correct ladder that's leaning against the correct wall. Only when both of these conditions are met, and at all times, is when you are on a path leading to your success.

After going through the process presented in this book, besides creating your executable Individual Development Plan, you will also be ready to answer those tough interview questions, such as: "Why should I hire you?" and "Tell me something about yourself." "What motivates you?" and "Where do you see yourself five years from now?"

You will be ready, as well, to respond to the question: "Do you have any question for me?" or "What questions do you have for us?" Both of those questions are usually answered, "No, not at this time," or with a slight smile and obvious nervousness, both of which show that you did not prepare or know what to ask, or how to ask it. Instead, after reading this book, you will be able to turn this opportunity to your advantage; you will be prepared to start "interviewing" the interviewer by asking questions that matter to you, questions related to your individual developmental opportunities and the programs that particular company offers. As you read this book and follow the steps, you will gain plenty of ideas and suggestions about what questions to ask and how to recognize the best answers.

Kevin Davis, a good friend of mine and better known as "Quality Guy" among his friends, was one of a select few people with whom I met and discussed this process and my intentions to write this book. As I shared with Kevin my passion for people development and I illustrated the steps of creating and executing an IDP, he nodded and stated, "The process and the book would be of great help to many professionals, including myself, as well as useful in my direct reports. I am most impressed with how simple each of the steps is. They are based on common sense while at the same time, they are unique and easy to understand and follow." Kevin got very excited when we finished the conversation and he said, "This book will make my job easier—from personal development as well as my ability to support my direct reports and for them to develop themselves." Not to say, Kevin was among the first one to get to read this book before it was published and employ this process with his team!

I found the best way to conclude this chapter was to use a quote from the venerable Sir Winston Leonard Spencer-Churchill. As you know, Churchill served two terms as the Prime Minister of the United Kingdom, the first-time during World War II and the second in the early 1950s. He once said, *"The era of procrastination, of half-measures, of soothing and baffling expedients, of delays, is coming to its close. In its place, we are entering a period of consequences."* From here, you should be able to extract many lessons, among which is the need to stop the procrastination of creating and executing your executable IDP, otherwise you will have to face career-related consequences. The good news is, by picking this book and reading it thus far, you have already started—so keep going. The best part starts with the first chapter in the next section.

# TIPS FOR YOUR 1:1 WITH MANAGER

## Before the Meeting
- ☐ Read all three chapters in Section I
- ☐ Schedule the meeting
  - o Invite: Your direct supervisor / manager only
  - o Subject: "Discuss Individual Development Plan: Intro"
  - o Objective: To inform your manager about your intentions of creating your executable Individual Development Plan and the process (steps) you plan to follow

*Recommendation: Schedule the meeting at least one week in advance*

## During the Meeting
- ☐ Inform manager about the reasons* you want to create you executable Individual Development Plan
- ☐ Seek feedback and input and manager's personal experiences
- ☐ Ask for permission to schedule periodic progress reviews and feedback exchange
- ☐ Share with your manager the book (provide him with his own copy) and process you intend to follow

*Recommendation: Give a copy of the book to your manager so that when you two meet, you can both be on the same page (pun intended)*

## After the Meeting
- ☐ Send summary of the meeting
  - o Remind the manager about the book, process, and next steps + express your appreciation (Thank You)

## Write Your Meeting Notes Here: _____

*\*Refer to Section I of this book for reasons "Why you must have an executable IDP?" and how this book / process can help you accomplish that*

# SECTION II

## The Solution: It Starts and Ends with an EIDP

# How to: **Create your** *executable* **IDP**

T
he proven process, as depicted on the next page, of creating and executing your executable IDP consists of nine distinct steps. These steps are laid out in a unique sequence representing the roadmap that guides you to successfully reach your full potential and achieve your career objectives. Furthermore, based on the activities associated with each of the steps, the steps are grouped into five states: EIDP, Future State, Decision State, Current State, and EIDP—hence, "*It starts and ends with EIDP.*"

The first state, the "EIDP" state, consists of a single step, called "Step 1: Make a conscious decision." This step, no matter how trivial, is an important first step. As with any process, taking and completing the first step seems to be the hardest. You may ask, "What is so hard about making a decision to do something you must do or want to do, anyway?" On the surface, you are probably correct, yet when it comes to making a decision that will ultimately impact your career—your ability to reach your full potential and your career objectives—then there are some essentials you should learn and pay special attention to. These essentials, together with questions and answers, are included in chapter, titled "How to: Make a conscious decision."

Following the "EIDP" state is the "Future State." The "Future State" consists of two distinct steps, "Step 2: Choose your career (NOT job!) path," and "Step 3: Perform the research." Both steps are forward thinking and future focusing. In the step two, you need to choose a career path among the three most common career paths, Subject Matter Expert (SME), Program Manager (PRM), and People Leader (PPL). Each of these career paths has its own pros and cons and each of them has its place in almost all organizations regardless of their size, industry, or geographical location. To better understand these career paths and to ultimately make an educated choice, read the chapter titled "How to: Choose your career (NOT job!) path." In this chapter, you will learn about each of the career paths, their places in the organizations, as well as be introduced to the templates and examples. This will help you successfully complete the step two and put you on trajectory for the rest of creation and execution of your executable IDP.

The step three, also in the "Future State," focuses on performing the research about your chosen career path. Of all the steps, this step can be most challenging and time consuming. But it is a right thing to do before moving any further into the process. In the chapter titled "How to: Perform the Research" you can learn about all the research that you should complete as well as how to complete it. At the end of this step, you will be ready to evaluate your career path choice. For this step, you should use a custom-created "Research Results Matrix" template, which will guide you to successfully complete this step as well as help you later, in step seven, to identify and acknowledge the gaps.

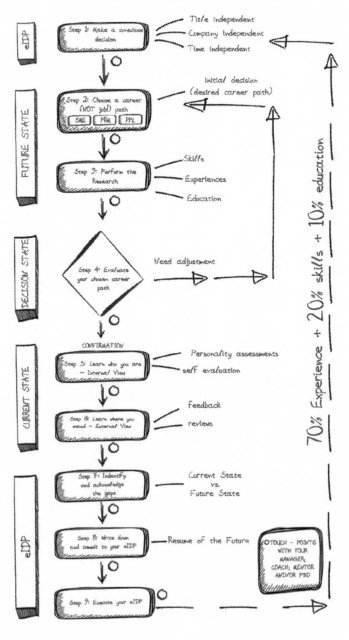

"IT STARTS AND ENDS WITH EIDP"

The "Decision state" is the third state in the process and contains one step—the step four, appropriately titled "Step 4: Evaluate your chosen career path." This is the most important step and state in the entire process of creating and executing your executable IDP. By extension, it is also one of the most important evaluations you will ever make in your career. To help you evaluate your decision, you should plan to take time to reflect, share your research findings, and consult with your coaches and mentors, as well as be honest with yourself. Furthermore, this is a step where professional help may be needed before you move forward. It is imperative to fully read and follow the guidance in the chapter titled "How to: Evaluate your chosen career path."

Once you have completed the steps one through four (which you may have to cycle through more than one time), you come to the "Current State." The "Current State" is designed with keeping "learning about yourself" in mind. In this state, you should complete a number of self-assessments, including but not limited to MBTi®, DiSC®, StrengthsFinder® as well as a number of feedback assessments, such as "360 degree" and Emotional Intelligence (EQ). To learn more about each of these internal and externals views and assessments, you should read these two chapters, "How to: Learn who you are—Internal View," and "How to: Learn where you stand—External View." With them, you would be able to successfully complete the steps five and six. Between the "Future State" (steps two and three) and "Current State" (steps five and six) you should have all prerequisites completed to successfully create and execute your executable IDP.

The last state in the process of creating and executing your executable IDP is the "EIDP" state. In this state you will spend most of your time compiling the information collected, analyzing, and acknowledging the differences between the "Future State" and the "Current State," and writing your executable IDP. Most importantly, in this state, you will also commit to your executable IDP as well as you will start with its execution. The step seven, "Step 7: Identify and acknowledge the gaps"; step eight, "Step 8: Write down and commit to your EIDP;" and step nine, "Step 9: Execute your EIDP" are all part of the EIDP state and should be fully completed in this order. To better understand what to do and how to do it, you should read the corresponding chapters: "How to: Identify and acknowledge the gaps," "How to: Write down and commit to your EIDP," and "How to: Execute your EIDP."

By following these steps, this proven process of creating and executing your executable IDP, either on your own or by reading the "How to…" chapters, you will end up with a personalized executable IDP that should help you reach your full potential and achieve your career objectives. To increase your chances of success, you should utilize the templates, tips, questions, answers, and examples provided throughout the book (and available on the website: www.jasminnuhic.com or www.myeidp.com).

# How to: **Make a conscious decision**

*This chapter provides explanation, examples, tips, suggestions, and tools that will help you successfully complete the step one, "Step 1: Make a Conscious Decision."*

Making a conscious decision is the very first step in creating your executable IDP. Yet, before making the decision it is important that you read this chapter all the way through and understand the three critical prerequisites for a sound decision. These three prerequisites are acceptance that your executable IDP must be created independently from any specific position title, independent from your current and any other employer (company), as well as independent from any specific time expectations.

Three prerequisites for sound decision are acceptance that your executable IDP must be created indenpendently from:

☐ Any specific position title  ☐ Current and future employer (company)  ☐ Specific time expectations

NOTE: If you agree, place a checkmark ✓ in the square ☐ next to each of the pre-requisites

This does not mean that, through the development of your executable IDP, you will not target a specific role within a company, or target a specific company to work for, or set some goals in terms of time. These will be outcomes of the process of creation and execution of your executable IDP—not inputs. Confusing? Let me explain and elaborate on each before we move forward.

## Prerequisite # 1: Independent from a Title

The first prerequisite, and perhaps hardest to accept, is that your executable IDP must be created with no specific job title in mind. This means it must be created as *title independent*. There are number of reasons why your executable IDP must be created with no title in mind. At this time, you will learn two of them: the executable IDP helps you build a career not a job, and different organizations (companies, industries) have different position titles for the same roles.

The primary goal of creating an executable IDP is to come up with a clear roadmap that would help you achieve your full potential and achieve your career objectives. For that reason, it must be based on your strengths, values, personality, and interests. Such an executable IDP goes beyond just single promotion (for example, moving from engineer to senior engineer, or from manager to director), or role change (for example, change from subject matter expert to a people leader, or from people leader to a program manager). It rather gives you a roadmap that encompasses all promotions and role changes necessary to build a successful, satisfying career. Besides, if all you want are the short-term results, next level job, or change of a role, then instead of creating an executable IDP, all you need is that position's job description. Once you have it, map your current qualifications against it and the gap between the two is your plan. This would be *very* shortsighted, the equivalent to driving a car by looking at your dashboard as well as stopping at every single intersection to ask yourself which way you should turn next—and then hope that the road you picked would lead you towards to your desired destination. Not an optimal means of travel.

The same is true when it comes to your career path. The other reason that creation of your executable IDP must be title-independent is that different organizations, companies, businesses, and industries have different titles for the same roles. This is also true for the same company that may have different job titles at different times for the same roles. Since you want to create *your* executable IDP, it means that the same IDP must be transferable across different companies (more about this later in this chapter under "company independent") as well as to be timeless— even within the same company (more about this later in this chapter under "time independent").

## Prerequisite # 2: Independent from a Company

The second prerequisite for a sound decision about creating your executable IDP is to accept that your executable IDP must be *company independent*. Of the three prerequisites, this one is probably most self-explanatory and easiest to accept. According to the Bureau of Labor Statistics and its most recent available data, which is based on monthly survey results of sixty-thousand professionals, the average worker today stays at each of his or her jobs for 4.4 years while the expected tenure of the workforce's youngest employees is about half that. At the same time, based on Future Workplace "Multiple Generations @ Work" survey of 1,189 employees and 150 managers, 91% of Millennials (born in the period between 1977-1997) expect to stay in a job for less than three years. This means they would have fifteen to twenty jobs over the course of their working lives! These job changes include changes of positions, companies, and industries, as well as careers. You may already relate to these facts from your personal experiences or know friends and coworkers that have experienced it. Given this statistic, the probability is high that you will change employer before you reach your full potential and achieve your career objective. For that reason, you should create your executable IDP that is applicable to your current employer *and* any future employer. As such, it is something that you will be able to take with you to your desired (next) employer, company, organization, or industry.

## Prerequisite # 3: Independent from a Time

Finally, the third and last prerequisite for a sound decision related to creation of your executable IDP is that your executable IDP must be *time independent*. Why time independent? Well, there are two elements to this. One being the time it takes to create your executable IDP. This can range anywhere between few weeks to a number of months. Professionals that are highly motivated and follow the steps presented in this book usually end up creating their executable IDP within a matter of weeks— some as quick as nine weeks. Others, due to number of different justifiable reasons (i.e. work, personal conflicts, lack of motivation, wrong expectations, etc.) end up spending closer to twenty-four months. The second element is somewhat harder to control and, ultimately, harder to predict. It is related to opportunities necessary to develop skills, get education, and gain required experiences. As you probably know already, opportunities come and go, so timing the creation and execution of IDP around opportunities can be difficult. On a positive note, such a thing is definitely not a show-stopper, yet it must be accepted as a prerequisite for a successful creation of your executable IDP. Later in this book, when we come to the steps where opportunities are needed, I will tell you ways that you can create opportunities and with that, somewhat, control the pace of creation and execution of your executable IDP.

With the prerequisites out of the way, it is time to talk about commitment and patience. Just like a diet, or exercise, or any other significant and meaningful assignment, commitment and patience are required. The good news is that both are challenged, and strengthen throughout this process, making you that much better of a professional. They—commitment and patience—also help you later with the execution of your executable IDP as well as dealings with any setbacks (I will cover more about how to deal, and avoid, setbacks in the last step). For now, all you need is to make a conscious decision to start working on your executable IDP—which is position title independent, company independent and time independent. And remember that the process of creating and executing your executable IDP is not a sprint; instead, it is a marathon. It is a marathon that lasts for an entire working life. Now, it is your turn to make a conscious decision to start working towards reaching your full potential and achieving your desired career objective—to start working on creation of your executable IDP.

# TIPS FOR YOUR 1:1 WITH MANAGER

**Before the Meeting**
- ☐ Read the Step 1 in Section II
- ☐ Schedule the meeting
  - ○ Invite: Your direct supervisor / manager only
  - ○ Subject: "Discuss Individual Development Plan: Step 1 - COMPLETED"
  - ○ Objective: To share with your manager your learnings in Step 1 and to inform your manager about your conscious decision to create an EIDP as well as to discuss next step (Step 2)

*Recommendation: Schedule the meeting at least one week in advance*

**During the Meeting**
- ☐ Share with your manager your learnings in Step 1
- ☐ Seek feedback, inputs, and manager's personal experiences, any company/industry insights and foresights, as well as names of the people to meet (build relationships / network with)
- ☐ Ask your manager about his/her thoughts on the process/book (given that they read the book)

*Recommendation: Encourage your manager to read the book and follow along (maybe have other team members involved as well)*

**After the Meeting**
- ☐ Send summary of the meeting
  - ○ Remind the manager about the next step (Step 2) + express your appreciation (Thank You)

**Write Your Meeting Notes Here:** _____

_____

_____

_____

# How to: **Choose your career (NOT job!) path**

*This chapter provides explanation, examples, tips, suggestions, and tools that will help you successfully complete, "Step 2: Choose your career (NOT job!) path."*

In this chapter, you will learn how to complete the second step of creation and execution of your executable IDP. You will also learn, through research, networking, and reflection about three different, unique, career paths, of which you will ultimately choose one. Yes, you can, and perhaps you will, change your decision in the future, but for now, you will need to choose one. These three unique career paths represent over 90% of all career opportunities—regardless of industry, organization, and level. They are Subject Matter Expert (SME), Project Manager (PRM), and People Leader (PPL). Each of these three career paths are respected, required, and desired in most of all organizations. They obviously serve different roles, which are explained in more details later, as well as they are key parts of any business eco-system. The remaining 10% of career paths are mainly consistent hybrids of two or three of the aforementioned career paths. They exist in smaller organizations and sometimes in volunteer-based organizations. Even though they are important, this book focuses on the three core career paths only. Once you have full understanding and knowledge of these core career paths, you can derive the hybrid ones.

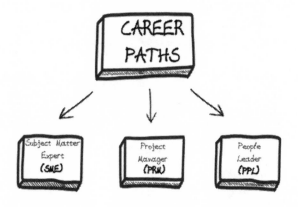

Let me describe the three core career paths: subject matter expert, project manager, and people leader in more detail.

**Career Path: Subject Matter Expert (SME)**

Subject matter expert, also known as an SME, as well as an individual contributor, is a career part that is full of roles such as engineer, salesperson, support/admin, programmer, business partner, specialist, consultant, advisor, assistant, and many others. They are, by definition, professionals with authority in a particular area, topic, subject, or domain. This career path, in its nature, consists of professionals interested in holding only themselves accountable and responsible. They prefer to work alone or to be assigned to a team. They always strive to reach their personal best, to discover something new, to achieve a breakthrough, to contribute directly through their own work (instead of through direct reports as it is in the case of people leaders, which is covered later in this step). In another word, SMEs are professionals that prefer the "road less travelled." As a career path, SME is applicable to professionals of all kinds of personalities (introverts and extroverts), types of people (left-brainers and right-brainers), personal backgrounds (Americans, Europeans, Asians, Africans, Australians, etc.). You, after some research, may find that being an SME is the best fit for you and of most interest to you when it comes to creating an executable IDP and reaching your full potential achieving your career objectives. Some of the known SMEs include Tim Berners Lee (developed the http:// protocol for the internet), Galileo (developed a powerful telescope), Thomas Edison (filed over one thousand patents), David M. Axelrod (senior advisor to the president of the United States), Elena Kagan (Associate Justice of the Supreme Court of the United States), Marjorie Lee Browne (noted mathematics educator from Memphis, TN), Yolande Cornelia "Nikki" Giovanni Jr. (one of the world's most well-known African American poets), David Cheriton (arguably the richest professor), to name a few. Note that these people sit on boards of both for-profit and non-profit organizations as well as serve as consultants to many presidents, vice-presidents, directors, and various media houses. They have invented life-changing devices or proved most difficult yet beneficial theories. Their knowledge, skills, and education are also part of organization's competitive advantage. Because of this, SMEs get called when key decisions are to be made, or when critical work is to be accomplished, or when credibility to a case needs to be added. Some SMEs become very famous, some very rich, yet as it is in case with those mentioned above, they were all successful and, most importantly, content with being SMEs. They are required for a team, organization, and business to be successful.

### Career Path: Project Manager (PRM)

Project Managers (PRM), which represent a family of professionals that include but not limited to project leaders, program managers, portfolio directors, and project coordinators belong to a second core career path. By the nature of their roles in organizations and businesses, PRMs mainly manage project related tasks and actions. They get work done through other people, primarily different types of individual contributors (SMEs). For this reason, PRMs, in order to be successful, must possess strong influencing skills, have cross functional knowledge, be very good generalists, and on top of everything else, have very strong business acumen. In comparison to SMEs, who normally have very enriched roles (roles specific to a function, area, domain, single expertise, and so like), PRMs have very enlarged role (general knowledge of multiple functions and areas while a lack of expertise to perform in any). Furthermore, in smaller organizations, PRMs are mostly hybrid roles consisting of having to be a combination of both SMEs and PPLs. Here are some examples of Project Managers that you either know or should know about: George E. Mueller, PhD (Project: Land on the Moon in 1960s), Chad Bowman (Project: Memphis Aerotropolis), Samuel C. Phillips (Project: Minuteman and NASA's Apollo Manned Lunar Landing), Lisa Watts (Project: GPS with real-time traffic info). And here are some of the products that are results of successful project management: battery for cars (Tesla, Prius, Volt), smart devices (phones, tablets, appliances), airplanes (Dreamliner, Airbus 380), rovers (Curiosity and Opportunity) and many more well and less known. Besides these well-known PRMs, there are countless PRMs leading projects related to medical devices, operational excellence, software and hardware development, and deployment, construction, as well as environment-health and safety improvements, grass-root movements, and many, many others. Nevertheless, PRM, as a career path, is respected, needed, and, in many cases, required for a business or organization to succeed.

## Career Path: People Leader (PPL)

The third and last, yet equally important and needed, career path is People Leadership or also known as PPL and people management. In this category of career paths belong positions and titles such as supervisor, manager, director, vice-president, president, and chief operations officer (CEO), which in simple terms means positions that have people directly reporting into them. PPL, as a career path, is perceived as the best, the most important, and the one where ultimately everyone should be. Wrong! As aforementioned, SME career path and PRM career path are just as important, needed, and required. Furthermore, PPL does not even exist without SMEs and PRMs. On top of that, according to the Center of Creative Leadership, 40% of people leaders fail within first eighteen months on the job while even greater number fail to meet the expectations of those that hired them or those that they lead. The reasons for those failures are numerous. Some of them are objective, yet a clear majority of them are subjective—meaning you have control over them. On a positive note, PPLs focus and hold control over their resource allocation and utilization, evaluate and improve performance, help their reports through coaching, and invest in self and team development (through creating, supporting, and executing executable IDPs). In a number of organizations and businesses, PPLs are doers and leaders at the same time. They also hold a much-enriched role. Some of the successful, arguably "Level 5" leaders, as Jim Collins defines it in his book *Good to Great*, are Warren Buffett (Leader of Berkshire Hathaway), Omar

Ishrak (CEO of Medtronic), and some others such as Angela Merkel (Chancellor of Germany), Christine Lagarde (Managing director, International Monetary Fund), Michael Bloomberg (Business owner), Dr. Shirley C. Raines (eleventh president of the University of Memphis), Fred Smith (founder of FedEx), as well as many directors, like Michael Sulek (Director of Quality), Dominic Presty (Director of Manufacturing), Michael Herringshaw (Director of Supply Chain), Carolyn White (Executive Director of Quality for Research and Development), Heather Savage (Strategic Sourcing Director, Advanced Sourcing) and managers, such as Mario Maricevic (Procurement Manager), and Lisa Hong (Environment, Health and Safety Manager).

After you read about these three—SME, PRM, PPL—core career paths, you should take a moment, a break, to reflect, think, and even talk to your mentors, family members, and friends about each of them. Then, choose one—one career path that you would like to pursue, and for which to create your executable IDP.

In the next chapter, "How to: Perform the Research," you will, through research, discover and learn of many education expectations, skills requirements, and experiences needed, to be successful PRMs, SMEs, or PPLs.

# TIPS FOR YOUR 1:1 WITH MANAGER

**Before the Meeting**
☐ Read the Step 2 in Section II
☐ Schedule the meeting
  o Invite: Your direct supervisor / manager only
  o Subject: "Discuss Individual Development Plan: Step 2 - COMPLETED"
  o Objective: To share with your manager your learnings in the Step 2 and to inform your manager about which career path have you chosen for yourself as well as to discuss the next step (Step 3)
*Recommendation: Schedule the meeting at least one week in advance*

**During the Meeting**
☐ Share with your manager your learnings in Step 2, research you completed and career path you have chosen for yourself and your reasons / thoughts behind it
☐ Seek feedback, inputs, and manager's personal experiences, contacts, information pertaining to the career path you have chosen
☐ Ask your manager for coach and/or coaching in the areas of chosen career path
*Recommendation: Encourage your manager to read the book and follow along (maybe have other team members involved as well)*

**After the Meeting**
☐ Send summary of the meeting
  o Remind the manager about the next step (Step 3) + express your appreciation (Thank You)

**Write Your Meeting Notes Here:** _____
_____
_____
_____

# How to: **Perform the research**

*This chapter provides explanation, examples, tips, suggestions, and tools that will help you successfully complete the step three, "Step 3: Perform the research."*

To get the most out of this chapter, you should at least read the chapter before: "How to: Choose your career (NOT a job!) path," and perhaps the chapter, "How to: Make a conscious decision." Nevertheless, with the decision in mind and career path at heart, it is time to perform the research. This step, the findings and results of your research, is of utmost importance of this entire process, and ultimately of utmost importance for you to potentially reach your full potential and achieve your career objectives. By the time you finish reading this chapter, and complete the work associated with this step, you will have a clear picture of the career path you have chosen as well as what it means to be successful within the scope of such career path. No worries, just as before, you will be guided along the way—this book will help you with tips, suggestions, ideas, guidance, concrete examples, and specifically designed templates.

The very first thing to do here in this step is to make a list of the people that you (and perhaps your mentor) think and believe are successful in their careers. Their careers shall be directly relevant to your chosen career path. For example, if you have chosen SME as your career path, then the list should be comprised of SME individuals, regardless of their age, gender, sex, ethnic background, or industry and company where they work. The only requirement is that they are very successful SMEs. On the same note, if you have chosen PRM as your career path, then the list should be comprised of individuals that are very best PRMs. The same is true if you have chosen PPL as your career path. Do not take this lightly. Take your time. Make a serious effort to do your best research here and come up with the list of best people possible. Remember, their experiences, education, and skills are what you will be looking for, what you will study, and, to a certain degree, try to replicate. At the end, your list should include at a minimum of three to five people (if you can do seven, that much better) from each of the following three circles: immediate circle, extended circle, and outside circle.

**Your First Circle: Immediate Circle**

Your immediate circle consists of people with whom you already have some level of relationship, personal or professional, established. These people include your colleagues, people that work with you at the same company or organization; your classmates and professors, people with whom you either have attended or are attending school, as well as the professors and instructors at the university; your club mates, people with whom you either have or still play sports, and coaches, and club leadership; your family and friends, people with whom you socialize or have family ties. All of them are candidates for your list, and you may be positively surprised of their experiences, education, and skills, which you never knew they had.

# YOUR CIRCLES

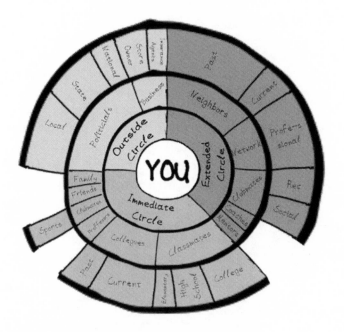

## Your Second Circle: Extended Circle

Your extended circle represents people from your social and professional networks. Social network, as the name implies, consists of people from your social circles, like people that you met through a common friend, people with whom you play recreational sports, members of your country club, and even your neighbors. All these people have potential to give information you may need during this research phase. Your professional network, even though it may be vast through social media, should be carefully analyzed for the selected few professionals that are either recognized by you or someone else as "successful"—successful as SMEs, or PRMs, or PPLs. These people should include your mentors (more about mentorship and the importance of mentorship later), people from your mentors' network, people from your managers' network, and members of professional organizations of which you are member.

## Your Third Circle: Outside Circle

Finally, people that come from your outside circle, meaning people that you do not know, nor do they know you, yet you know of them and you deem them appropriate to be included. A quick tip: yes, even people that do not know you, most of the time, are willing to help you for as long as you meet these four criteria: 1) you approach them with respect for their time, education, experiences, or skills, 2) you offer them something in return, which may include reimbursement of some sort, 3) you promise (and deliver on the promise) to follow up with them with the outcome of their input, and 4) ensure them of absolute confidentiality. And always *thank* them! These individuals, regardless of gender, industry, religion, race, age, and company, may include Doctor of Philosophy (i.e. your professors), politicians (i.e. local, state, federal), business owners (i.e. insurance agents, store owners, or manufacturing), chairpersons (i.e. from non-profit organizations), and CEOs (i.e. of company where you work). Nonetheless, engaging your outside circle is by far most challenging and delicate process, yet the potential return on this investment makes it well worthwhile—definitely worth trying.

Once you have identified the individuals from each of the three circles—immediate, extended, and outside—create a matrix of their names, contact information, most notable education, experiences, skills, and how you are connected to them (i.e. common friend, or references from the network) as well as any other comments that would later help you recall. Make sure you leave extra space next to each person where you will populate the outcomes of the research, such as questions and answers, references, links, and more. This matrix will ultimately end up being a "Research Results Matrix" (full version available for FREE to download from the book's website: www.myeidp.com or www.jasminnuhic.com) and will serve as input into the Step 4, "Evaluate your chosen career path," and later again in the Step 6, "Learn where you stand—External View."

## BONUS TIP:

Professional organizations are usually a nonprofit organization seeking to further a particular profession, the interests of its members and community at large.

With the "Research Results Matrix" completed and ready, the next task is to gain understanding of what to research. As mentioned before, there are three specific requirements for successfully reaching your full potential and achieving your career objectives. They are: what to learn (education), what to master (skills), and what to have (experiences). Some would argue, and I would agree with them, that there is a fourth requirement: Business Acumen. More about business acumen at the end of this section (also see the Bonus Tip).

**Research Area: Education**

Let's start with education. Etymologically, the word "education" is derived from the Latin word *ēducātiō* meaning "breeding; bringing up; rearing." It is a process of acquiring knowledge, being taught, most commonly, at a formal school or event. Education is highly theoretical and conceptual in nature, yet at the same time very important, and sometimes a gating prerequisite for the other two requirements: skills and experiences. It is also the easiest one to research and understand as well as to obtain.

---

## BONUS TIP:
Use "Research Results Matrix" to establish your (initial) Personal Board of Directors (PBD)—the ultimate network

---

Furthermore, education is very broad, so understanding what kind of education is needed for your career path, what level of education is required, recommended, and desired, as well as to what extent continuous education is expected, can save you a lot of time and money, and most importantly, keep yourself focused. Of the three requirements, education contributes roughly 15% of the overall creation and execution of your executable IDP. For that reason, you need to update your "Research Results Matrix" with questions pertaining to education, and whom to ask which question. Remember to include some of the same questions to multiple individuals in order to generate trends and confirmations. There is so much more to be said about education, and so you will come back to it later in the book.

### Research Area: Skills

Next, let's dive into the skills. Skills directly relevant to your chosen career path contribute approximately 25% to the overall creation and execution of your executable IDP. Just like education being the single most important prerequisite for the other two requirements, so are the skills the single most important element in being successful in your current and future roles. When researching skills needed to be successful within your chosen career path, make sure you include questions related to people skills, hands-on skills, technical skills as well as tools associated with each of the skills. Skills can be harder to understand and even harder to gain. To get the most out of your research, when gathering the information from your contacts, make sure you include mostly open-ended and follow-up questions. Even better, if and when possible, seek to observe and experience those skills. The good thing with skills is, as you research them, you can simultaneously apply them in your current role—and with that harvest short-term and long-term benefit from them. Meaning, use the skills you are learning for success in your current role as well as start getting ready for the next one.

### Research Area: Experiences

Last, yet hardest to research and gain, is experience. According to Etymology Dictionary, "experience" dates back to the sixteenth century and has both Latin and Old French roots. Its meaning is "experiment, proof, trial, practical contact with, and observation of, facts or events and knowledge gained by repeated trials." Experience contributes the entire remaining 60% of the creation and execution of your executable IDP. Yes, it is that important! While researching experiences of your contacts

50

from all three circles, prepare and ask questions related to the roles they served, geographies they lived in or traveled to, challenges they worked on or managed, situations in which they have been involved, decisions and lessons they learned (try to get them to reflect earlier in their career, to dig deep), and people with whom they worked.

When receiving the responses to your questions, make sure that you pay special attention to time commitments (i.e. work hours), travel requirements, assignments, pros and cons of their chosen career path, personal stories, impact to social life as well as overall recommendations and passions. For you to get the most out of the research, your questions should trigger all of these in all of the people from all three circles in order. Again, ensure the same questions are being asked to multiple people and look for trends and other analytical opportunities. Word of advice and caution: no matter what (or how much of) experiences you have, they all matter. Do not assume that you already have all of the needed experiences. They all may seem trivial, but they all are significant. Finally, the best thing about experiences, which is different from both education and skills, is that all experiences are good, and all can be leveraged during creation and execution of your executable IDP.

**Research Area: Business Acumen**

As mentioned before, let me touch on Business Acumen again. For most people, business acumen represents working knowledge of finance and accounting, yet business acumen is far more than that. Overall, business acumen is ability to see the big picture while acting on details. It is being able to understand how you, your decisions and actions, impact the organization, especially when expected to "think on your feet." Depending on the organization, your chosen career path, and level in the organization you serve, having a strong business acumen can be anywhere between 10-50% (in some cases more) of expectations and requirements. So then, why do I not have business acumen as a separate fourth requirement to research during this step? The reason is that business acumen is part of education *and* skills *and* experiences. The expectation is that your chosen people will share with you level of business acumen you need to have to be successful in your chosen career path. If they do not, then ask. In parallel to asking, I would also highly recommend reading the book, *What the CEO Wants You to Know: How Your Company Really Works*, by Ram Charan, a world-renowned business advisor, author, and speaker who has been working with many top companies, CEOs, and boards of our time. You may check Ram's YouTube video named "Ram Charan: The Shopkeeper Mentality" for a quick introduction and overview of the business acumen.

---

## BONUS TIP:

Wikipedia defines Business Acumen as keenness and quickness in understanding and dealing with a business situation in a manner that is likely to lead to a good outcome.

---

Up to this point, you learned how to approach performing the research from people identification standpoint as well as what to seek out from them. Now, you will move into the "how and where" part of the research. Remember, when it comes to the research, the outcome and results of the best research are high-quality data. After the research, the data gets analyzed and conclusions are made, and that is exactly what will be covered in the next chapter "How to: Evaluate your chosen career path." If you were scanning through the previous sections of this step, now is the time to slow down, take a deep breath, and have your "Research Results Matrix" available to take notes. That is how you will get the best data and results of your research and, with that, conclude this step in the process of creating and executing your executable IDP.

Let's go back to our three groups of people that come from three different circles: immediate, extended, and outside.

---

## BONUS TIP:

When conducting a research, think like a lawyer and act like a journalist—always be ready to ask that "one extra question"

---

When it comes to the people from the immediate circle, the research should be focused mostly on gathering the data through in-person interviews and observing them in their regular daily activities. In addition to it, and whenever possible, the research should be focused on shadowing them through some key events and reading relevant documents and records. In-person interviews lead to best results when they are scheduled, and questions are planned and communicated in advance. Also, contrary to mainstream thinking, the in-person interviews produce better data and results when conducted in the interviewee's regular work environment (instead of coffee shop or during lunch at a restaurant, or even a barbeque at your place). The same is true for observing and shadowing. The exception is, when it comes to shadowing, not everything can be predicted, yet strive to conduct it during a regular workweek (instead of when special events are scheduled). In addition, there should be time allocated

---

for individual reflections—you alone, and collective reflection—you and your contact together. These reflections would give you time to update the "Research Results Matrix," plan and schedule the next steps, and most importantly, give you a chance to ask clarification questions, which you may not have been able to ask before. Understanding that your immediate circle, and people you selected from the immediate circle, are close to you and they know you, you should feel most comfortable with them, and them being comfortable with you. This should lead into the most substantial research. Maximize the research from the people from the immediate circle before you move into the next step—reaching out to the people from your extended circle.

The people you selected from the extended circle may be harder to reach and get any time in person, however, whenever possible, it should be done. At least you should strive to meet them in person, even if that means driving longer distances to see them. Just to make a point, I have both driven long distance (approximately six hundred miles) to see one of the people from my extended circle, as well as have coordinated an extra-long flight layover to meet another person from my extended circle. Both times, every penny and minute invested in it was worth it. The best alternative to meeting in-person would be video-telephone, such as Skype and Face-Time (or any other tool available). If this is the route you choose, be reminded that the same rules as for in-person interview apply to the video-telephone interviews. This means that you have to make sure that you maintain proper eye contact, that you keep away distractions such as email and phone; take notes on paper instead of typing (but this can come across as disrespectful and annoying as well as it would prevent you from making eye contact), smile and maintain a proper posture. Besides these rules, additional tips apply, such as ensure proper lighting, web camera placement, extra attention to your nervousness, test your connection, check your background (make sure it is appropriate), and finally, look at the camera instead of the screen. What I would discourage you to use with the people from your extended circle is any type of text-only communication: email, text message, or software.

At the end, these people are from your extended circle and they are borderline helping you, and your appreciation for it may be lost in text-only communications. Again, you want to get most out of your contacts from the extended circle before you move to the people from the outside circle.

---

## BONUS TIP:

Do not forget traditional research method: reading! Read about people from your career path—in newspapers, magazines, autobiographies, academic books, and papers, etc.

---

People from the outside circle, as defined at the beginning of this chapter, are people that you have a long shot of reaching and even longer shot of receiving any responses from. I do not mean to discourage you. Just to set the right expectations and maybe even challenge yourself to prove me wrong. It would only be better for you, in short- and long-term. With the people from your outside circle, you should try to have an interview, either in person (these people are usually very much worth driving, even flying, to see them) or via video-telephone. However, in the absence of being able to do that, here are other options: write them an email with your questions, follow them and contact them via social media, sign up for their blogs and (inter) company newsletters, or ask your mentors, managers, and other contacts if they can help you get introduced to them. In any case, whether you contact them directly or through your contacts, make sure you always thank them for their time, expertise, and input. Lastly, when everything else has been exhausted, read the job descriptions of the positions and roles that are directly in your career path. Read these job descriptions regardless from what industry, geography, or company they come. Look for information and requirements pertaining to education, skills, and experiences—from both the required section and desired/optional section. The data / information which comes from the job descriptions will help you fill into the blanks where you may have data missing from all other research.

At the end, know that there would be people you selected from all three circles who are not responding to your requests, or you feel you are not getting the most out of them. It is okay! Still thank them, and then select another person from the same circle and try with her or him. The focus should be on the goal, which is data and results, and if that means you need to spend more time, or talk with more people, so be it.

Once you get this far, you should have the research completed and your "Research Results Matrix" should be completely filled out. That would be a sign to move to the next step, "Step 4: Evaluate your chosen career path." Keep moving; you are halfway there to having your own customized executable IDP in place.

# TIPS FOR YOUR 1:1 WITH MANAGER

## Before the Meeting
- [ ] Read the Step 3 in Section II
- [ ] Schedule the meeting
  - o Invite: Your direct supervisor / manager only
  - o Subject: "Discuss Individual Development Plan: Step 3 - COMPLETED"
  - o Objective: To share with your manager your learnings in Step 3 and to inform your manager about the research you completed as well as to discuss the next step (Step 4)

*Recommendation: Schedule the meeting at least one week in advance*

## During the Meeting
- [ ] Share with your manager your learnings in the Step 3, research you completed, and conclusions you have derived from the findings (perhaps, share your "Research Results Matrix")
- [ ] Seek feedback, inputs, and manager's personal experiences, contacts, information, thoughts, comments, ideas, etc.
- [ ] Ask your manager for any additional information that either complements or corrects your research/findings

*Recommendation: Invite your manager to read some of the research that you have completed*

## After the Meeting
- [ ] Send summary of the meeting
  - o Remind the manager about the next step (Step 4) + express your appreciation (Thank You)

## Write Your Meeting Notes Here: _____
_____
_____
_____

# How to: **Evaluate your chosen career path**

*This chapter provides explanation, examples, tips, suggestions, and tools that will help you successfully complete the fourth step, "Step 4: Evaluate your chosen career path."*

This is a crucial step in the process of creating and later executing your executable IDP. In this step, you will either confirm or correct the decision you made in the step two (Step 2: Choose a career (NOT job!) path) and with that you will either move into the step five (Step 5: Learn who you are—Internal View) or go back to the step two (Step 2: Choose a career (NOT job!) path). I will explain this later, but for now let me first introduce what happens in this step.

For this step, you need to book some "me place" and "me time"—a place and time where and when you can work alone. Preferably, you should book multiple working sessions that last a couple of hours each. The reason for it is that in this step you will be doing a lot of reflection, analysis, and if necessary, more research. This will ultimately lead to decisions. You do not want to take this lightly. Also, in this step, you will use the "Research Results Matrix," which you created in the previous steps,

58

as the main tool and guide. By using the "Research Results Matrix," you will be able to analyze and reflect on the data that is supportive, and data that is conflicting with your chosen career path. This is the emotional part of this step. In addition, you will be able to analyze and reflect on the data in order to recognize "the known" as well as to acknowledge "the unknown." And that is objective part of this step. Let me elaborate and provide guidance on each.

Either you are using an electronic or hard copy version of the "Research Results Matrix," I would strongly suggest arming yourself with several pens, highlighters, sticky notes, stickers, and symbols of different shapes and sizes (may be more favorable for people that have challenges seeing or distinguishing colors). Once you have everything ready, open the "Research Results Matrix" and start looking only for the data that is *supportive* of your career path decision.

**Analyze and Reflect On: Supportive Data**

Supportive data is the data that came out of research as highly energizing to you. This means what you heard, saw, and read about the career path is putting a smile on your face, giving you a reason to daydream, and most importantly, it is giving you the energy to continue. In other words, supportive data is the data that makes you feel good about your decision and you see yourself spending the rest of your career life learning about it and doing it at work. Furthermore, the supportive data can be recognized through reflection as well. Reflect on the time when you were gathering the data, either through in-person interviews, by observing and shadowing someone, or simply reading someone's response to your questions, and you felt excited and maybe even passionate. All that data, identified through analysis and reflection, is confirming your decision about the chosen career path and should be marked and grouped together. At the end of this step, hopefully, this group of data would be the largest. Yet, for now, keep the bias at bay. When you get to this point, then stop. Take a break. Or, even better, end this session and schedule the next one—for the next type of analysis and reflection. Experience tells me that this break should be at least a day or two.

## Analyze and Reflect On: Conflicting Data

The next analysis and reflection should be directed towards *conflicting* data, meaning the data that conflicts with your chosen career path. This is hard to do as we humans have a heavy bias towards our decisions and way of thinking. So, you must be conscious of this and periodically check yourself by asking to what extent your analysis and reflection is biased towards your already made decision. Again, this is hard, and thus conscious effort is required. With that said you should go through all of the data in the "Research Results Matrix" and start marking the data that conflicts with your chosen career path. This data can be recognized through analysis, simply by considering the trends of negative information gathered during the research. It can also be recognized through reflection. By reflecting on your data-gathering and the time when you were hearing or reading the data—the time when you asked yourself, "really?" or when you felt that what you were reading or hearing was demoralizing and energy draining. On top of that, look for data that may be in contrast with your personal values. This requires meaningful reflection and honest self-questioning. You may find out that a piece of data, or whole trend, conflicts with one of your core personal values, which you would not be willing to compromise.

Let me share with you my personal example on this point. Early in my career I worked on perhaps one of the highest visible projects initiated by the company's CEO: implementation of the new, company-wide, Enterprise Resource Planning (ERP) system. As you can imagine, this project contained a number of large and small projects and I was responsible for one of them. I was very excited and felt both challenged and rewarded. I also had to work long hours, which I did not mind; had to travel a lot, which I enjoyed; was given many perks, which I appreciated; yet at the end of the project and, ultimately the overall program, I had decided that I never wanted to do it again. Such career path was not for me because it violated one of my core personal values—family quality time. This became apparent one night when I came home after long hours at work. I ate dinner and then worked some more. A few minutes before midnight, I finally went to my bed next to my wife, and that is when I heard an email arriving to my phone. The lights in the room were out so I tried to feel for the phone with my hand. Nevertheless, my wife heard it, and made a single comment, "You aren't going to do it, are you?" That was the moment I realized that I had been compromising my personal value, family quality time. I also realized that in order for me to be successful in the long run, I needed to change my career path. I went back to the step two, "Choose Your Career Path." If you have a similar story or, through analysis and reflection, you can predict the same story happening to you (in your chosen career path) you may want to consider going back to the step two. I did it, and you can do it, too. Once you have completely analyzed and reflected on the data, as well as marked and grouped the conflicting data in the "Research Results Matrix," it is time to take yet another break. Another day or two long breaks, before moving forward.

With the emotional part of this step behind you—completed analysis of supportive and conflicting (what some people may call "pros and cons") data, it is time to put the emotions on the side and focus on the objective part of this step: *recognizing the known* and *acknowledging the unknown.*

## Recognizing the "Known" and Acknowledging the "Unknown"

When it comes to recognizing the known, the task for you here is to, once again, go over your "Research Results Matrix" and mark or otherwise highlight all the data representing what you already know or have. This means, as you go over the data, identify all skills, education, and experiences which you already know and have, yet also matches your chosen career path. For example, let's say that your chosen career path is PRM, and your research data shows that a successful PRM holds a certification from an accredited body such as Project Management Institute (PMI). And let's say that you already have taken the PMI certification exam and passed it. This would be a match, and this would be something you already have. As such, you should highlight or otherwise mark it. On the same note, if your chosen career path is SME, perhaps the research data yielded that some strong practical skills in one of the statistical analysis software is required. And again, let's say that you have already gained these skills throughout your education and work. You should once more highlight, or otherwise mark, this as something known to you. Finally, along the same lines, if your chosen career path requires experience with budgeting process (beyond your household budget) and allocation of resources (primarily people, direct reports), and you have gained such experience via your current or previous role, then you would recognize this as something known and mark it as such. It is important to be honest with yourself and not stretch your skills, education, and experiences just to make them fit. It is absolutely okay, and to a degree desirable, that you are short of the requirements. This would further motivate you to grow. It would further explain to you why you are not there yet—when it comes to fulfilling your full potential and reaching your career objectives. This reminds me of C-Jay and my encounter with him.

I met C-Jay after one of my speaking engagements. He was a quiet man, well dressed, in his mid-forties. He was also very frustrated from lack of progress towards his career goals. He felt that the time was running out on him. Later, he and I (on his disappointment and excitement at the same time) found out that the source of his frustration was he himself. After my talk, C-Jay approached me and flat out said, directly and right after saying his name, "Jasmin, I want you to help me find a way for others to recognize what I know." As soon as he said it, I picked up on the words, "*others* to recognize" what he knows. With a level of surprise of his directness and his plea for help, the first thing that came to my mind was to ask him, "Do *you* know what you know?" He replied, "Of course!" and then he proceeded telling me his entire resumé. No joke! He talked for more than fifteen minutes straight. All the while I was trying to take mental notes. Remember, I was not ready for this and had no pen and paper or my computer readily available. In fact, I was packing it all after my talk. By the time he was done, the others that wanted to talk with me were long gone, the host of my talk was ready to leave, and, quite frankly, I was tired and ready to leave, too. But then I realized that C-Jay is a person I can, and I should, help with creating his executable IDP. At the end of the rundown of his resumé, I promised C-Jay that I would help him.

The following week, we kicked off the process, the process being described in this book. When we arrived at this step: step four, it was only then that he realized what he wanted "others" to know, he did not know himself. Not only that, but also what he had told me during his resumé rundown, he realized that his education was at par with the requirements of the successful career path, yet his skills and experiences were significantly short. As I mentioned, he was both disappointed and excited at the same time. In another word, he had an "a-ha"[2] moment. The good news is that C-Jay stuck with the program, and without any more a-ha moments. He recently called me and reported, "I am now on my path toward reaching my full potential. I'm very content with the progress I've made toward achieving my career objectives." He continues to work on executing his executable IDP and, in the process, continues to learn about himself (you will cover this in great deal of depth in the next step).

---

## BONUS TIP:

Make conscious effort to actively seek feedback as well as pay attention to unsolicited (constantly happening) feedback.

---

Finally, this step comes down to identifying, highlighting, or otherwise marking, any and all of the *unknowns* to you. As always, you need to use your "Research Results Matrix," and to look for data and information you heard for the first time, or even heard about it before yet never took time to learn, or much less master. I suspect that this group would be the smallest, with the least amount of data. It will be, certainly, one that would take most of the

---

[2] Concept derived from the book "From Success to Significance: When the Pursuit of Success Isn't Enough," by Lloyd Reeb

time and effort to master, to address, in order to get closer to reaching your full potential and ultimately achieving your career objective. Once you have identified and marked the unknowns, you may have some data left unmarked and ungrouped in your "Research Results Matrix." That is okay. It happens to most people and the question always comes up as what to do with it.

First, if you truly followed the initial instructions and took your time to complete each section of this step separately, with some intermediate breaks, and also if you made sure that you scheduled the time (instead of rushing it or doing it ad-hoc) to spend in a private and quiet area, you probably would not have any data left. In fact, you would potentially end up thinking that you still have some questions that need to be answered, and with that, more data to be generated. This is what happens to that minority of people who strive to get the most out of this process the first time around. But do not worry, you probably still have enough data that you can move forward, so just go ahead and group the remaining data together with the unknown group. This would ensure that you cover all your bases and later end up with the most comprehensive executable IDP. That is a good thing! It is time to take yet another break before moving to the last two sections of this step, which are: sharing your data analysis and revising or confirming your decision about your career path (the decision you made in the step two).

With your data analysis done. With your reflections completed. With the groupings and markings on your "Research Results Matrix" done. Your next duty is to share it all with your family, trusted friends, managers (see end of this chapter for tips), and most definitely your mentors. This is the critical moment, where you should seek and receive honest and open feedback about your research, your analysis, and your reflections. This would provide you with a direct feedback on how they relate to, or support or conflict with, your decision about to your career path. Feedback is a key for this and each of the following steps in creation and execution of your executable IDP. Without feedback, you would have the same chance for reaching your full potential and achieving your career objective as a pilot of a commercial airline flying blind. Yet, most people do not seek, do not know how to seek, feedback. Furthermore, they do not even know how to recognize and benefit from the unsolicited feedback. Since there are many well-written books and other materials on the topic of receiving and giving feedback, I will only share with you some of the key elements here. At the same time, I would suggest you pick some of those books and materials and read them. Most of them do a very good job complementing this book.

Here are top three key elements related to feedback:

1. *Prerequisites for effective feedback* are, at minimum, trust between the person giving feedback and the person receiving the feedback, respect for the individual, positive intent, focus on the ultimate goal, time, and timing, and always being consistent.

2. *Elements of feedback exchange* consist of the process that starts and ends with the recipient. It goes as follows: the recipient (i.e. you) asks for both specific appreciative and specific constructive feedback, the giver provides specific (i.e. using examples) appreciative feedback first, followed by the specific (i.e. using "I" statements) constructive feedback second, and lastly provides additional details—further narrative. The recipient acknowledges receipt of the feedback and thanks

the giver. It is also highly recommended to include an extra step, which is follow-up with the giver— for either further clarification and/or to share how the feedback was used.

3. *Do's and Don'ts of receiving and giving feedback* include but not limited to, **do** focus on behavior and actions not the person, **do** provide specifics, **do** be empathetic yet direct, **do** be timely (and spend time), **do** exchange feedback in the right setting (place), **do** focus on a single message, **do** be open and honest, **do** be factual, and **do** provide content. **Don't** use generic and absolute terms (i.e. always, never), **don't** "attack" the person, **don't** judge, **don't** make it personal, **don't** give unsolicited feedback, **don't** discredit the good, and **don't** do it in public.

You have reached the last section of the step four, and the second of the two decision points in the process of creating and executing your executable IDP. By this time, you should have gone through your entire "Research Results Matrix;" you should have received trusted and open feedback; and most importantly, you should have evaluated and gauged the decision you made in the step two against all of that. Now, the question on the table is, "Should you go back to step two and revise your decision, or should you go to next step and continue with the already made decision?" You are the only one that knows the answer to this question. Yet, if you are still uncertain, still debating, and need one more tip from me, then here it is: If the research you completed in the step three, and analysis and reflection of data you completed in the step four, does not violate any of your personal values, something that you are not ready to compromise for anything, including your career, then continuing to the next step makes sense, otherwise, going back to the step two would make more sense. Going back to the step two would add time required for creating and executing your executable IDP, yet it is the investment you want to make now. It is also the wrong decision you want to correct before you go too far in this process and your career. On the other hand, if you are moving forward with your original decision, then keep reading on about the step five, "How to: Learn who you are—Internal View." This step is perhaps the most interesting step in the entire process of creating and executing your executable IDP.

# TIPS FOR YOUR 1:1 WITH MANAGER

## Before the Meeting
☐ Read the Step 4 in Section II
☐ Schedule the meeting
  - o Invite: Your direct supervisor / manager only
  - o Subject: "Discuss Individual Development Plan: Step 4 - COMPLETED"
  - o Objective: To share with your manager your learnings in Step 4 your evaluation, and any changes related to your chosen career path as well as to discuss the next step (Step 5 or back to Step 2)

*Recommendation: Schedule the meeting at least one week in advance*

## During the Meeting
☐ Share with your manager your learnings in Step 4, and your (re)evaluation of your chosen career path
☐ Seek feedback and any additional information and updates since previous conversations, as well as encourage your manager to challenge your (re)evaluation and the next steps
☐ Ask your manager who else you should share your (re)evaluation with, as well as for any current and upcoming opportunities that fits your chosen career path

*Recommendation: Check with your manager if/who else may be or should be following this same process of creating and executing their EIDP*

## After the Meeting
☐ Send summary of the meeting
  - o Remind the manager about the next step (Step 5) + express your appreciation (Thank You)

## Write Your Meeting Notes Here: _____
_____
_____

# How to: **Learn who you are—Internal View**

*This chapter provides explanation, examples, tips, suggestions, and tools that will help you successfully complete the step five, "Step 5: Learn who you are— Internal View."*

In this step, you will look at yourself in a mirror, a virtual mirror, that is. In this mirror, you will be able to see far more than just the color of your eyes, clothes you are wearing, and your good looks. Instead, you will get to "see" your internal features invisible to a naked eye. Confusing? It should be. Let me walk you through it. First, you will spend some time finding ways to see yourself internally, through number of scientifically and statistically sound self-assessments, such as Gallup's StrengthsFinder™, MBTI®, DiSC®, and some others. These would be followed by spending some time finding out how others see you, through such tools as 360° Feedback, One-on-One feedback, performance reviews, and assimilations.

Depending on your chosen career path, there will be some additional specific tools that are relevant to each of the career paths (all this and more in the next step of this process). And this is not all. You will also be reaching out to your manager and mentor and seeking additional means of seeing yourself and learning about yourself. Still confused? Do not worry; it will be fun, as this step is truly the most interesting step in the entire process of creating and executing your executable IDP. It is so interesting some people, like C-Jay (and me too), continue to come back to it past the initial creation of the executable IDP. We continue to find new ways, relevant ways, to learn and see ourselves from various perspectives.

---

## BONUS TIP:
To get most out of any self-assessment, feedback, tool, and/or assimilation, you have to trust the process of that tool.

---

You probably noticed, and already asked yourself, how come the Intelligent Quotient (IQ) self-assessment has not been mentioned at all? Since this is a typical standard self-assessment that most people complete at least once during their school age, I wanted to make this self-assessment optional. Please do understand though, if you have never completed the IQ self-assessment then please do so at this time. It will help you find out if you are a logical thinker, or numerical whiz, or verbal genius. Similarly, it will help you find out if you are spatially inclined, intellectually challenged, as well as how "smart" you are. The best news is, by taking the IQ self-assessment you increase your intelligence. Plus, it measures your logical reasoning, math skills, language abilities, knowledge retained, and the ability to solve novel problems. It does not tell you how well you perform under stress (there is no time limit for the self-assessment) or take into consideration your emotional intelligence (later in this step, there is a dedicated self-assessment for emotional intelligence, one of the single biggest predictors of performance).

According to the Office of Career and Professional Development at the University of California, San Francisco, learning about yourself, seeing yourself in the virtual mirror, is important because it "is the key first step in navigating your career. It's your ability to reflect and articulate your values, interests, abilities, and personality preferences. Your responses will be the criteria you use to evaluate the pros and cons of different career paths and jobs." This is so true and complements the famous Confucius' statement "*Choose a job you love and you will never have to work a day in your life.*" Yet to achieve that, in order to find a job that you will love, and ultimately be successful in, you need to learn enough about yourself and to learn how others see you. These statements, regardless how incomplete, very well summarize the reasons why this step is built into the process of creating and executing your executable IDP. Besides, no matter the extent of the research you have completed thus far, and career path you have selected, if you lack knowledge about yourself, your skills, your education, and/or your experiences then how do you know that you are on your way to reach your full potential and achieve your career objectives? Again, in this step, you will focus on learning about yourself through three main means: personal assessments, professional feedback, as well as review and reflection on your already gained education, skills, and experiences (your resumé).

But before you dive deep into the details, let me also elaborate why this step is a part of the process of creating and executing your executable IDP. Why is it this late into the process, and more importantly, how it fits into the short and long term of your journey towards reaching your full potential and achieving your career objectives.

The reason that this step is part of the process of creating and executing your executable IDP is to inject some reality into the process. Meaning, up to this point you have been daydreaming, looking into the future, thinking about the big picture, meeting with important and significant people, as well as "seeing" what you *will* have. This step brings you back to reality and helps you discover what you *now* have. Nevertheless, the differences in mindset, and ultimately the difference between the *will have* and *now have* are the basis for putting your executable IDP in writing. Trust me, this is a necessary step, and a step in the right place at the right time, It is also a step that may take the longest time to complete, yet it will be an interesting and fun time.

Along the same lines, the reason that this step is the step five, instead of step four, or step three, or any other earlier step, is to prevent you from boxing yourself into a career path that, based on your *current* education, skills, and experiences, may be a best fit. Let's take a look at Monique, for an example. Monique, a female professional, is classified as a minority based on her heritage and background. She was one of the people I got to know over time. She spent most of her professional life working within the scope of a career path that was not suitable for her. Now, past her middle-age and at the tail end of her professional life, she is working as a freelance software architect, being a subject matter expert. But this was not always the case. Monique, in her early twenties, finished college with high GPA (grade point average) and number of extracurricular activities. Being a female and minority in a mostly conservative environment, she had to work hard and fight for herself on a constant basis. This helped her to develop resilience, patience, a strong work ethic, and it motivated her to study hard. On top of that, in order to get out of her comfort zone and prove herself, she was always on the lookout for opportunities to volunteer, do extra work, and build relationships. At times, this was a taxing task. "Coming out of college and joining the workforce, I carried those skills, education, and experiences into my first job as a position of a Project Manager for a mid-size company in Federal Drug Administration (FDA) regulated industry. I thought this was the right start, the right fit, as I got a title of manager. It was great because I was able to employ most of the skills, education, and experience I'd gotten up to that point." The start of the job career, was good, yet over time, the progress became slower and slower. For her, to be successful was getting harder and harder. Monique continued trying to prove herself to herself and others, while the numerous professional feedbacks she received and her self-assessment results pointed towards a direction of an SME—instead of PRM. A direction that shows that she would be more successful in the role of an engineer, programmer, or consultant. "After a number of years of increasing struggles in the role of project manager at my first company, I changed companies and slightly changed jobs—I became a people manager in a project management office (PMO)." The same continued. She continued to struggle to be successful while the feedback was consistently pointing to a role of an individual contributor. "Finally, at my third company—third career path—I found happiness, balance, success, and a true calling." She became a software architect in a small information technology department of a large healthcare company. This role is an individual contributor role, and serves as an SME. Today, at the tail end of her professional life, she enjoys her work with full passion, makes a lot of money, has a healthy work-life balance, and enjoys mentoring young and upcoming professionals. She focuses on minority female professionals that work on their career paths (she plans to use this process to complement her lessons learned).

By now, you may see how this step fits within the process of creating and executing your executable IDP. What you may not realize yet is that this step alone brings additional value to the process as well as you. For the sake of this book, and this process, I will focus on the short-term value, yet at the same time I will mention some of the long-term benefits that you should keep in mind.

In short-term, the value comes from finding your current skills, education, and experiences which will further help you with picking the right career path and identifying the gaps between what it means to be successful in that career path and where you currently stand. You will be able to see this as you start completing the assessments, collecting the feedback, and reviewing your achievements and accomplishments. Likewise, in short-term, the additional value of this step is that you will be able to apply everything you learn immediately, and in some cases, in real-time.

As for the long-term benefit, you would have to be patient. In long-term, you will be able to undertand how to work with others, build relationships, benefit from different personalities, and recognize changes in yourself (and those around you) over extended periods of time. By this, you will be able to accommodate, adjust, and adapt to different circumstances that would always keep you ahead of most other people.

Last but not least, before you dive deep into actions, you should know what this step should produce—what are the expected results of the actions you will take in this step. The first, the obvious, result is that you will learn to see yourself in a mirror in a much different way. The second result of your actions will be a clear understanding of where you are in the journey towards reaching your full potential and achieving your career objectives. You will be able to identify your current strengths, weaknesses, your personality type, your preferences, and your biases. You will see what others think of you and how they perceive you—you will become aware of your blind-spots. The third, and perhaps most directly related outcome of this step, is that you will be able to crystalize your knowledge of your skills, education, and experiences. Consequently, you will gather many pieces of information about yourself and so I recommend that you create a "Personal Profile Matrix." This matrix is available for FREE to download on the book's website www.myeidp.com or www.jasminnuhic.com and can be used as a centralized file where you will record the results of the personality assessments, professional feedback, and information from your current resumé. You will learn more about each as you dive deep into the details next. Ultimately, your "Research Results Matrix" and your "Personal Profile Matrix" will be the two inputs into the gap analysis and creation of your executable IDP. Now, let's dive into the details and actions of this step.

Although you can start with any of the three areas, personality assessments, professional feedback, or analysis of your resumé, or even with all three in parallel, my experience suggests that the best place to start is with the personality assessments. For that reason, in this process I will start with the personality assessments. Personality assessments are many. In this step I will cover a number of them, keeping in mind that you can find many more on the book's website or simply performing an online search. Those included in this step, most likely, will be sufficient for the creation of your executable IDP. As you execute your executable IDP, you may want to complete additional assessments. In this step, I will introduce an assessment, provide you with a short description and explanation of the assessment, provide you with the instructions how to obtain them, and what results and/or outcomes of each assessment you should expect. As always, my goal is to help and guide you through this process to the extent possible while the expectation is that you drive and own the process. Remember, personality assessments are internal views of you in front of the virtual mirror, therefore the more focused you are, the better view you will get.

## Personality Assessment: Myers-Briggs Type Indicator®

To begin the personality assessments, you will start with the Myers-Briggs Type Indicator® or more commonly known as "MBTI®" or "that personality test." This assessment traces the patterns in your behavior to one of sixteen distinct personality types and gives you a framework for understanding yourself and appreciating the differences in others. As stated before, only when you really see yourself in the mirror is when possibilities open for you—in all aspects of your life, including professional. Upon completion of the MBTI ® you will get a detailed report of your personality type (one of the sixteen mentioned above) preferences, and most likely feel energized and challenged at the same time. Depending on the version of the test, your results may also include careers and occupations most suitable for your personality type. The test uses letters representing four personality preferences, one from each of the four preference pairs— Extraversion (E) or Introversion (I), Sensing (S) or Intuition (N), Thinking (T) or Feeling (F), and Judging (J) or Perceiving (P). These preferences help indicate how you focus your attention, what energizes you, how you take in information, and how you process and use that information to make decisions. It also helps indicate how you deal with the world around you. Thanks to the Myers and Briggs Foundation, Isabel Briggs Myers, and her mother, Katharine Briggs, MBTI® self-assessment is readily available. It is interesting to note that the results of MBTI® may never change—they stay constant throughout your life. At least with me, I have taken different versions of this self-assessment within the span of over ten years and the results were just about identical each time. What is more interesting with the MBTI® test is the way it works. The test is timed, which adds significant pressure to respond to each question and statement quickly, yet responding to each question and statement is not required. Correspondingly, the questions are structured in so-called "forced-choice," which means that you have to choose only one of two possible answers to each question. The choices are a mixture of word pairs and short statements. Choices are not literal opposites but chosen to reflect opposite preferences on the same dichotomy. For the best results and to get the most out of MBTI®, make sure that you read and follow all instructions very carefully. Again, once the test is completed, you get a detailed report of your personality type, which you should record in your "Personal Profile Matrix." I would suggest sharing the results with your mentor and partner immediately. Because I have personal experience with the MBTI® test, I do not think that you need any professional facilitation in order to complete it and get greatest value out of it. Instead, just take your time to prepare and strive to respond to as many questions and statements as possible. For your convenience, the link to the MBTI® self-assessment is included in the "References and Resources" section of this book and also available on the book's website.

## Personality Assessment: StrengthsFinder™

The next self-assessment that you should complete is connected to discovering your strengths. According to Gallup, Inc., an American research-based global performance-management consulting company was founded in 1935. This test is based on a forty-year study of human strengths and it is called "StrengthsFinder™." Originally published in the early 2000s, StrengthsFinder™ contains a list and descriptions of thirty-four unique strengths, of which, based on the self-assessment, five are identified as top strengths. It is designed to provide not only your top five strengths, but also number of nuances of what makes you unique on a professional and personal level. According to the StrengthsFinder™ validation and published information, even though you and a friend may both have the same top five strengths, the way they manifest themselves may not be the same. Therefore, each person receives entirely different, personalized, descriptions of how the strengths operate in their lives. "These new Strengths Insights describe what makes you stand out when compared to the millions of people [that they] have studied." StrengthsFinder™ is definitely one of the most researched and recognized self-assessments and there is no wonder that it made it into the process of creating and executing your executable IDP. Besides being such a well researched and validated assessment, it has been envolving over time. The original assessment was good, yet since the original publication, the Gallup organization has improved the assessment and made it both faster and more reliable. The way the assessment works is that you are presented with 180 questions / statements and twenty seconds per question / statement to respond to—it is a timed self-assessment. The response options are "strongly agree," "agree," and "neutral," where you are strongly encouraged not to respond with "neutral" in many cases (this is so that the results are more focused). It is an electronic self-assessment and the results come immediately after you complete the assessment. When it comes to the results, if you take the StrengthsFinder™ self-assessment multiple times, you may get slightly different results—meaning, your top five strengths tend to change over time. This is expected; as you learn, grow, and develop over time, your responses become different, ultimately leading to different set of strengths. For example, when I took the StrengthsFinder™ self-assessment the first time, my top five strengths were responsibility, achiever, analytical, belief, and focus. When I took it a second time about seven years later, my top five strengths were learner, focus, futuristic, analytical, and achiever. Notice that the three out of five of my top five strengths remained the same. As it is the case with the MBTI®, for the best results, be disciplined about following the instructions and trusting the process as this assessment, based on the Wall Street Journal, Business Week, and USA Today bestseller book, can dramatically change the way you look at yourself in the mirror. To find this self-assessment, I would recommend going directly to the main source—to the Gallup's StrengthsFinder™ website, order the book (make sure you get the most recent version, which as of this writing was *StrengthsFinder 2.0*), and use the code from the book to access the self-assessment (on the same website). This way, you will ensure that your results are generated with the most current information, and relative to all others that have completed the same assessment. For additional examples of the assessments, feel free to browse the internet or visit a public library. Similarly to MBTI®, professional facilitation of this self-assessment and interpretation of the results is not required. As a matter of fact, the team from Gallup has done a tremendous job including all necessary explanations in the results report as well as provided additional resources on their website. At the end, after you complete the assessment, review the results and the report. Also, update your "Personal Profile Matrix" and share the report with your manager and your mentor (even with your family members and peers).

## Personality Assessment: DiSC® Profile

The next self-assessment that I would recommend using, to better learn about yourself and your preferences, to see yourself in the mirror, is DiSC® Profile. This unique and widely available self-assessment is all about professional life. It is a way to improve yourself through improved performance, increased productivity, and enhanced communications. Although the results of this assessment may apply to personal and social lives, the main objective is to become more successful professionally. As such, the DiSC® Profile self-assessment fits perfect into the process of successfully creating and executing your executable IDP. There are many good things about a DiSC® Profile self-assessment starting with the fact that it is non-judgmental and produces a detailed personality report which tells you which of the four behaviours is your dominant one. The four behaviours are **D**ominance, **i**nfluence, **S**teadiness, and **C**onscientiousness. On top of all that, the DiSC® Profile self-assessment is one of the easiest and simpliest self-assessments out there. The way it works is that professionals like you respond to a number (approximately forty, but this could vary depending on the assessment) of statements instead of a single word. The responses are on five-point scale, known as the Likert Scale. In general, the assessment can be completed relatively quickly—in some cases, ten minutes or less. Note: there are literally tens if not hundreds of different versions of this assessment, of which some are free, some cost money, some validated and come with full reports while others give you only a high level feedback. My recommendation is to seek out the validated one (look for small 'i' in DiSC) as well as do your due-diligence before taking the assessment. Remember, the results matter as they influence your executable IDP and ultimately your career path. Speaking of results from the DiSC® Profile self-assessment, they include identifying your basic patterns. There can be between 15-160 patterns, and provide you with your dominant behaviour, which can be one of the following four: dominance, influence, steadiness, and conscientiousness (some results have "compliance" instead of conscientiousness). For your convenience, I have included direct access to at least one DiSC® Profile self-assessment that is known to be validated. You may find others on your own by browsing the internet or attending one of the leadership courses. Given that no professional facilitation is required, you can complete this self-assessment at any time of your convenience and place. The results of this assessment should be included in your "Personal Profile Matrix," and at least, be shared with your managers and mentors. I would also recommend sharing them with you subordinates and peers.

**Personality Assessment: The Rainbow Personality Test**

Subsequently, after a DiSC® Profile self-assessment, I would suggest taking the "The Rainbow Personality Test." As its name says, it is a test that tells you which is your dominant color, representing your personality type. The colors of this test are red, blue, yellow, and green. Later, when I talk about the results of this test, I will explain each, but for now let me tell you more about "The Rainbow Personality Test" itself. This self-assessment is based on Dr. Carol Ritberger's (a world-famous behavioral psychologist and author) hypothesis that states that there are four distinct personality types in the world: red, blue, yellow, and green. According to Dr. Ritberger, we all can be sorted into one of them. Because these personalities are exhibited in our personal and professional settings, knowing which color, which personality type you are, is a part of discovery necessary to be made to have a better, more representative, executable IDP. The way you can discover your color is to complete one or more (out of many) The Rainbow Personality Test self-assessments available. This self-assessment is by far the shortest and easiest (and arguably the most fun) to complete, yet the results can be very impactful and eye opening. For example, by completing a simple seven-statement self-assessment, which you can find online, it will already give you a good idea which color of the rainbow you are. Of course, a more detailed (over thirty statements) self-assessment will produce results that are more statistically sound while at the same time raise awareness of yourself. This is true even as you are completing the self-assessment. The reason for this is the way this particular self-assessment works. The way it works is that you should fully read each of the statements, take a short time to reflect on each, and then respond by, in most cases, agreeing or disagreeing, or in some cases, frequently or infrequently. Understanding this, I would highly recommend having a quiet time and place to complete this self-assessment. For the best results, make sure that you read and follow all instructions that come with this self-assessment. Again, when it comes to the results, they are very simple—you will receive a report stating your dominant rainbow color. In short, the colors represent the following: red - effective, optimistic, goal oriented, energetic, dominating and hotheaded, the best and successful; yellow - full of ideas, flexible, impulsive, and not following the rules and procedures; blue - persistent, stable, speculative, conscientious, and focused on stability and safety; and green - bureacratic, sceptical, prefer order and stability. On top of that, the natural tendencies of the people with these colors are: red - results, decisions, and challenges; yellow - optimism, impressions, and communication; blue - order, analytics, and discipline; and green - supportive, loyal, and consistent. It is important to note at this time that each and every one of these personalities have room in our professional and personal lives. They are all important parts of the overall world fabric. What is even more important is that each personality, color of the rainbow, has an equal chance of creating and executing an executable IDP, and with that, reach full potential and career objectives. As mentioned before, The Rainbow Personality Test self-assessment is easily found online and can be completed in either electronic or paper format. One thing that is different from all other self-assessments is that I would recommend sharing your results with your family members, perhaps your partner, first. Only after having this conversation and reflecting on the feedback, then share it with your managers and mentors as well as update your "Personal Profile Matrix." Beyond this, no professional facilitation is required, and for the most part, I would discourage it. Your best feedback and benefit should come from your immediate family member—your partner.

**Personality Assessment: The Seven Stories Exercise®**

"The Seven Stories Exercise®" is perhaps one of the most proven and longest lasting self-assessments available. The exercise itself has been adapted by the research community, practitioners, and professionals, as well as some of the most reputable publishers and management schools. The technique behind the "The Seven Stories Exercise®" is based on the work of Bernard Haldane, who, in the 1940s, worked with the U.S. government, asssisting military personnel to transition their military skills to public (civilian) skills. His success received the attention of Harvard Business School and it has been carried all over the world—from South Africa and China, to the Unites States, Canada, and Europe at large.

## BONUS TIP:

Given that each assessment is independent of another, hiring a coach to help you analyze AND synthesize the results as whole is recommended.

More recently "The Seven Stories Exercise®" was published and promoted by the *Five O'Clock Club* and *Breaking the Bamboo Ceiling*, a book written by Jane Hyun. I got to be familiar with both of these two sources and, for your convenience, I have included direct links to them in the resources section of this book.

"The Seven Stories Exercise®" helps you examine your accomplishments, looking at your strongest and most enjoyable skills. Given that it is based on the actual writing of stories and deep reflections, it is one of the most demanding self-assessments. It lasts days, if not weeks. Yet at the same time, rest assured that many busy professionals, including executives, make the time and effort to complete this self-assessment, and so if they can, you can too. With that said, there is no reason to worry, as "The Seven Stories Exercise®" comes with already developed and proven worksheets, which provide the necessary guidance in order for you to get the most out of it. In short, the way this self-assessment works is described next.

First of all, you are asked to make a list of all the enjoyable accomplishments of your life. Try to get at least twenty-five of them. To make it easier, reflect on all aspects of your life from work to recreation, from current age to your youth and school years, as well as any additional social elements, volunteer work, hobbies (very important!), and things which, every time you think of them, put a smile on your face. Note that these things do not have to be success stories, or even big accomplishments, they just need to be enjoyable, for you. The second thing is a bit tougher than the first. This is where you have to select exactly seven out of the twenty-five stories you have written down. The third thing is even harder as you are required to rank them in the order of importance and relevance to your pleasure. The list should then be numbered from one through seven. The fourth thing is to take each of the seven, in order, and write at least one solid paragraph about each one of them. The fifth, and last, thing is to dive deep into the analysis of those paragraphs and find a common core among all of them. For this, I recommend using help, starting with your friends and family but then also hire a professional, a coach that can assist you. Note: this self-assessment goes both in depth and width, and so having someone trained and experienced to help you is needed.

· When all done, the results are truly worth every second invested and every penny spent. You will walk away significantly closer to being ready to start closing the work related to creating and executing your executable IDP.

**Personality Assessment: Plus Specific One**

No matter which career path you selected, Subject Matter Expert (SME), Program Manager (PRM), or People Leader (PPL), all of the self-assessments introduced and described above are applicable, fully useful, and beneficial. Yet, at the same time, they are general and leave one single gap, and that is they are missing specifics related to your selected career path. For that reason, I suggest to all of my clients and audience at large, to complete at least one specific self-assessment related to their career path. Hence, "Plus Specific One." This self-assessment should be carefully picked as there are many available for each of the career paths. I would suggest talking with your mentors, managers, and peers (worst case, browse and research on the internet) to find out if they have a recommendation, an experience, with any particular one, and then take it.

There is only one requirement here: any self-assessment you select shall be designed for your selected career path, industry that you prefer to work in, and the results should be solely based on your inputs and responses. Stay clear of assessments that provide results based on any interpretation, or someone else's inputs and opinions. On top of that, it would be a bonus if the results are delivered immediately after the completion of the self-assessment and can be shared with people in your immediate, extended, and outside circles.

Remember: after you complete each of the self-assessements, make sure you update the "Personal Profile Matrix" with the results and outcomes as well as any related notes and comments. Again, your "Personal Profile Matrix" is a key for successful creation and execution of your executable IDP.

# TIPS FOR YOUR 1:1 WITH MANAGER

**Before the Meeting**
- ☐ Read the Step 5 in Section II
- ☐ Schedule the meeting
  - o Invite: Your direct supervisor / manager only
  - o Subject: "Discuss Individual Development Plan: Step 5 - COMPLETED"
  - o Objective: To share with your manager your learnings in the Step 5 and gain feedback about your Internal View as well as to discuss the next step (Step 6)

*Recommendation: Schedule the meeting at least one week in advance*

**During the Meeting**
- ☐ Share with your manager your learnings in the Step 5, and results of your research about your Internal View (perhaps, share with your manager your "Personal Profile Matrix")
- ☐ Seek feedback and any additional information and updates since previous conversations as well as encourage your manager to share his thoughts about your Internal View
- ☐ Ask your manager whom else should you share your results about your Internal View

*Recommendation: Encourage your manager to read and complete activities in this step—and share back with you (and the team)*

**After the Meeting**
- ☐ Send summary of the meeting
  - o Remind the manager about the next step (Step 6) + express your appreciation (Thank You)

**Write Your Meeting Notes Here:** _____
_____
_____

# How to: **Learn where you stand—External View**

*This chapter provides explanation, examples, tips, suggestions, and tools that will help you successfully complete the step six, "Step 6: Learn where you stand— External view."*

In the previous chapter you learned how to successfully complete and document the internal views. In this chapter you will learn how to complete and document your external views. As you probably realized, the internal views are 100% based on your own responses, which, inherently, you cannot argue with or dispute. It is different with the external views, as the external views are 100% based on how others see you. This can be tricky as how other people see you is always tainted with their own lenses, meaning *"people see you as they are, not as you are"* as stated by Sara Larkin in her work from 1986. On top of that, some people will argue that perception *is* reality. By default, this creates arguments and internal struggles, especially when their views of you are significantly different and conflicting with your view of yourself. Nevertheless, your success, in large part, depends on how other people see you and for that reason it is imperative to gain that knowledge in the process of creating and executing your executable IDP. Here is an example where one's self perception and perception of others were at odds. It is the case of a professional named Tah. Tah was an emigrant into the western world where he joined a small commodity manufacturing company. As one of the few employees, he was required to wear different hats and work on anything that needed to be done. He did not mind it; as a matter of fact, he enjoyed it and thrived by it. For that reason, he was perceived as a hard worker committed to the success of the company. As the company grew, its value and position in the market grew with it. Just like many other such companies, this company was acquired by a large international company, based out of northern Europe. After the acqusition, the company grew even more, and with the growth, the roles in the company became more specialized, the expectations became higher, and the results were measured on overall performance—instead of individual contributions. At that time, it became clear that Tah started to struggle. Primarily, it became obvious that for all this time with the company, yes, Tah was working hard, yet from the sea of things needed to be done, he was picking and choosing where to focus his effort. In the new structure and the new way of doing business, he was expected to work on things that the team and company needed him to work on. Tah continued to perceive himself as a high contributor while his boss and his peers saw him as a low performer and poor team member. Tah's career started to deteriorate. Despite a number of feedback sessions over the span of few years, Tah continued to ignore the views of others. At the same time, he continued to believe that he was doing the right thing. He also continued to expect promotions and recognitions in which he once was showered. Unfortunately, for Tah, it never happened. At the time when I got to meet with Tah, he was reaching the tail end of his professional life. I noticed that his view of himself versus the view of him by his peers and superiors was so vastly different that the opportunities for Tah to reach his full potential and achieve his career objectives were almost non-existent.

---

## BONUS TIP:

No philosopher using deduction or researcher using brain scans has been able to prove with certainty that our perception of the world matches "reality as it is out there."

---

Tah is not the only one with such or similar professional faith. Unfortunately, many young professionals start their careers on a very positive note and impress people around them. Some even reach the "high potential" status, yet they fail to create and execute an executable IDP that captures that moment and projects them to the successful future. For a second, think about yourself and your own start of the professional life, and where you are today, and ask yourself, "How much positive (or negative) impact, on my career, have other peoples' opinions about me?" Do not worry about coming up with the answer as you are about to find it through completion of number of external view assessments described below.

### External Assessment: 360° Feedback

The German-born, all-around and multi-level feedback-generating tool, is best known as 360° Feedback (read: three-hundred-sixty-degree-feedback). According to Wikipedia, it was originaly started by the German military in World World II, yet it was only in the 1950s that was used in public domain—first by Esso Research and

---

Engineering Company. It took another forty or so years before it started to be a part of the mainstream feedback tool. Today, 360° Feedback is arguably the most frequently used and most widely spread tool in the corporate, private, public, and non-profit organizations. It is said that, thanks to the easy access, primarily via online, it is used by thousands of professionals and volunteers around the world each day. For your convenience, I have included means to access the 360° Feedback in the "References and Resources" section of this book.

The way 360° Feedback works is simple yet profound. The fundamentals behind this tool are people that work all around you. Envision a ball, instead of a ring, and you are in the middle of it. Meaning it collects feedback about you from sample of people that work with you. Each of the following groups of people are sampled: your peers, your direct reports, your superiors, and other people with whom you interact, which may include customers, suppliers, and business partners, as well as the people with whom you may be on a project. This can be a challenging task since special attention must be paid to relationships. Nevertheless, all of these people are sent the same survey, with the same questions, as well as a copy of the sruvey is sent to you, for you to complete. The idea is that each and every corespondent (excluding you) anonymously completes the survey by responding to all questions and sends them to either your manager or mentor or coach, depending on your organization and your goals. The trick, and perhaps the most difficult task with 360° Feedback, is to come up with "the best" questions, since the questions need to be objective, timely, relevant, and specific, yet general as well as open and close-ended. The good thing is, with a little luck and careful timing, you can have 360° Feedback created and executed, and results collected within less than two weeks!

The results themselves—though they can be influenced by a number of factors, including but not limited to, number of people completing the survey, timing of the survey, quality of the questions asked, and trust factors—are still exceptionally useful in creating and executing your executable IDP as well as reaching your full potential and achieving your career objectives. The results, at minimum, provide you with information such as your perceived behavior, listening, planning, and goal-setting, as well teamwork, character, and leadership effectiveness. On top of that, most tools available today will provide you with a detailed analysis between your responses versus the responses of the people that completed the survey (again, the responses are all anonymous), give your narrative feedback details (from those that wrote in answers or provided clarifications on rated answers) and even suggest a development plan—inputs into your overall executable IDP. As before, for the best results, quality results, make sure you follow any and all instructions that come with the 360° Feedback tool and seek assistance where uncertain. Note that most of the time, and I would say well over 95% of the time, you only have one shot to get the best results. So, make sure you take your time to select the right tool, right people, and right timing.

360° Feedback tools can be found online, and also in the "References and Resources" section of this book. The one that I have included in there is well balanced between the investment and return, yet you may want to consult with your manager or mentor as they may have experience (or license) for yet another version of the 360° Feedback tool. What I would say though, the 360° Feedback should be taken very seriously and respectfully to your manager and mentor and people that are completing the survey for you, and as such most often requires a level of professional and independent help. My team and I can help as we not only have experience with administrating the 360° Feedback but also helping you incorporate the results into your overall executable IDP. Nonetheless, an independent person is required to help so that the confidentiality and trust of maintaining anonymity is preserved throughout the entire process and beyond. Finally, when it comes to the results, make sure you enter them into your "Personal Profile Matrix" and save them for future references and baseline.

**External Assessment: Emotional Intelligence (EQ)**

I cannot think of a better tool—a better way to gain external views, and at the same time complement the 360° Feedback—than Emotional Intelligence or EQ assessment. For that reason alone, you should complete the EQ assessment and feedback next. So, what is *emotional intelligence* (EQ) in the first place and how it is different than the intelligence quotient (IQ)?

Well, for starters, according to the American dictionary, emotional intelligence is a noun. It is "the capacity to be aware of, control, and express one's emotions, and to handle interpersonal relationships judiciously and empathetically." Also, based on the work published in *Emotional Intelligence 2.0* by Travis Bradberry, *"emotional intelligence is the key to both personal and professional success."* In contrary to IQ, which can only be exploited and expressed at different levels throughout your life (due to the limits being predermined by your genetics), EQ can be learned and enhanced at any time. To enhance your EQ and to increase chances for reaching your full potential and achieving your career objectives, you have to learn it. You can learn it by attending a traditional classroom, hiring a professional coach, or simply reading about ways of enhancing EQ and then reflecting upon it. Besides this, there are many other differences between IQ and EQ, yet they all boil down to the fact that EQ represents "soft" skills, such as the ability to control feelings and reactions as well as read other people's reactions and responses, while IQ represents "hard" skills including logic, math, and reading comprehension. Granting that both EQ and IQ are important; if you have never taken IQ, I would suggest you do take it and find ways to benefit from the results. The rest of this section is focused on the EQ. You are expected to complete this feedback assessment in order to create and execute your executable IDP. So, let's dive into how the EQ feedback assessment really works. EQ works around basic areas which include self-awareness, self-regulation, social skill, empathy, and motivation. These basic areas are also grouped into four categories such as self-awareness, self-management, social awareness, and relationship management. Of the four categories mentioned, perhaps self-management and relationship management are more "self-developed" and easier to master. Self-awareness and social awareness may be a bit more difficult to develop and may require more time. For these two, I would suggest soliciting help from your peers and relatives as they should be able to provide you with real time feedback necessary to master these skills.

When working on the EQ feedback assessment, know and understand as well as accept, that both the tests and results are somewhat subjective and hard to measure. Even though a number of tests have been developed, and some of them completed by millions of people around the world as well as the results directly compared to the success of those same people that completed them, there are still nuances related to your personality. For that reason, and for the sake of your time and effort in creating and executing your executable IDP, I would recommend securing the book *Emotional Intelligence 2.0* by Travis Bradberry, from TalentSmart, and completing the test that comes with the book, called *Emotional Intelligence Appraisal*. This test provides you with comprehensive results that "pinpoint the strategies that will increase your emotional intelligence the most and tests your EQ a second time to measure your progress." Again, as before, make sure that upon completion of the test, you record your results into your "Personal Profile Matrix."

---

## BONUS TIP:

Remember the quote from John Templeton, who said, "It is nice to be important, but it's more important to be nice."

---

The best place to find this book and the test that comes with it, is to contact TalentSmart or browse your favorite books-selling vendor, physical or virtual. Disclaimer: even though I do recommend the work of Travis Bradberry and the book *Emotional Intelligence 2.0*, I have no vested interest in either, and the recommendation is solely based on personal experiences and feedback from the professionals with whom I have worked.

In closing, when it comes to the EQ test and feedback assessment, you should share your results with your mentors and coaches, and albeit professional facilitation is not required, a deep reflection before, during, and after individual and group interactions is absolutely required.

## External Assessment: 1:1s

One afternoon, while I was leaving my office for an extended weekend with my family, Phillip, a friend of mine whom I met and graduated from business school with, called me all frustrated and ready to quit his job. "Jasmin, I am ready to quit my boss." Though the words were said with solid determination, it wasn't long before I realized he was not really ready to quit, but he sure was very frustrated. On the other side, I was already checking my brain out and started thinking about all the water slides I was going to slide on with my kids, and I was in a mood for jokes and smiles. Phillip was not having any of it. As a matter of fact, the first question that he asked was, "Can you teach me 'that program' you have for developing and growing? I want to grow out of my current role and my boss as soon as possible!" Again, I laughed and told him that "the program" is not something I teach, yet rather I share, and professionals just like him and many others, follow in order to develop their executable IDPs. Their executable IDPs, in turn, ultimately help them achieve their full potential and reach their career objectives. His reaction was, "Please teach me; I will pay you." At that moment, I realized that he was serious and more importantly, the conversation was about to turn sincere. Fortunately, I was still in my office and had my notebook available, and so we started. By asking Phillip the source of his frustration and urgency to learn "the program," he told me that he just had yet another, 1:1 (read: one-on-one) with his direct manager, and yet again he felt he did not get anything out of it. He did not know what to do next, in particular, about the project he was working on and his career growth opportunities overall. I forgot to mention, Phillip manages strategic projects, which are usually those that deal with "things never have been done before," or things of "high sensitivity / high confidentiality" in nature.

---

He was, at this time, still an individual contributor with an office on a top floor, a desirable salary, and a few additional attractive fringe benefits. Given that the frustration was the outcome of the 1:1 with his manager, I started with probing questions about that impactful 1:1 meeting. Phillip told me that his 1:1s are a waste of time and that he never gets any feedback on his performane and his development. So it was the case at this time. With a few more probing questions, and us going back and forth on what Phillip said versus what his manager said, as well as what were Phillip's expectations—before the meeting and during the meeting—I started to build the picture. A picture that represented comments of many professionals that seemed not to get the most value out of their 1:1s— either they be with their managers, mentors, coaches, peers and even subordinates and co-workers in general. They all, including Phillip, missed the implied and indirect feedback that they were being gifted with because they were expecting explicit, direct, and, in some cases, desired feedback.

---

## BONUS TIP:

Most common question I get, related to 1:1s, is: "How often should I have 1:1s?"
At least once a month—more importantly, it must be convenient and agreed upon with the other party (i.e. manager, peer, mentor, etc.)

---

You may be scratching your head just about now trying to understand what I mean by implicit and indirect feedback, and why am I calling it "a gift" and what that all has to do with having 1:1s. Or, you may also be scratching your head reflecting on your most recent 1:1 with your manager. In either case, the answers are coming. Keep reading.

1:1s are yet another key for developing and executing your executable IDP. They should be conducted with your manager—at the minimum, your peers and co-workers and, if you have direct reports, with them too. 1:1s should also be conducted with your mentors and coaches as well as your friends, especially if they work for the same company as you do—at least in the same industry as you do. When you are having these 1:1s, first of all, do not expect that everything will be shared in the first place, and of things being shared, not everything will be shared expliciticly and directly. Many messages will be communicated implicitly and indirectly through stories, examples, body language, and sometimes even time or timing of the 1:1. For that reason, it is crucial that all your senses, plus your best critical thinking skills, are turned on and paying attention. It is those senses and outcomes of the critical thinking that would give you an idea, and give you a gift, give you the feedback on how you are performing. They will also give you an idea of your developmental and growth opportunities. Make sure you record those notes and include them into your "Personal Profile Matrix" so that you can start recognizing patterns. The patterns will come if you record the same messages from various 1:1s from various people with whom you have them.

Back to my friend Phillip. After our extended conversation, which kept me in my office for another two-and-half-hours, he not only calmed down but more importantly realized that he indeed did get some constructive and appreciative feedback. The same 1:1 was of value to him. By the end of the conversation, Phillip was smiling and ready for the weekend while I was all back into working mode and forgotten all about the water park and water slides. I am happy to report, though, that the conversation was also the first session of many, where "this program" helped Phillip. By the way, he never paid, yet he continues to benefit from "the program" and from his 1:1s.

**External Assessment: Performance Reviews**

Performance Reviews, especially when done right and done frequently, are one of the best ways to capture the external views of you, and with that let you know where you stand. Just about all of the professionals working in the corporate environment that I have worked with, dislike, to put it mildly, performance reviews. We tend to think of them as useless and a waste of time. We tend to complete them and treat them very superficially. What a wrong thing to do. The only people these professionals are hurting by not doing their best job possible is themselves.

One time, the company where I worked was going through a major (this is understatement) reorganization. The decision was made to go from decentralized business management to heavily centralized and co-localized management. This resulted in a number of early retirements, lay-offs, changes to the reporting structures, new positions created, and many of the existing positions eliminated. I was anxious to find out if I would have a position and what would it be. I have to say though that I was told that I should not worry, yet seeing people being impacted all around me, it was hard to believe it. About halfway into the restructuring and reorganization, I met with my mentor and expressed my anxiety. By now, my mentor had known me for over ten years and at some point in time, we worked together in the same function. His words back to me were simple and direct, as he told me,

"What you have to worry about? Do not even update your resumé. If they decide to eliminate your role, just print out your past Performance Reviews and take them to any competitor and you will get a job immediately." Being true or not, I may never find out. Those words sure did put me at ease, and from that point on, I was far more relaxed. Quite frankly, I enjoyed the remaining of the reorganization and restructuring process. As a matter of fact, instead of being paralyzed by it, I was able to learn from it. You may think that the words of my mentor was what impacted me in a such a positive way. No! It was the fact that I could indeed rely on my past performance reviews to potentially get my new job.

I have always put in a serious effort in writing and reflecting on my performance evaluations. Regardless if they were done annually or quarterly, formally via system, or less formally via paper, or what my manager may think of them. I took my time to document the "whats"—what I have accomplished during the period, and the "hows"— how I reached those accomplishments. Just for an example, I once executed a project with a full scope, two weeks ahead of schedule and over 35% below the budget. It was a tough eighteen-months-long project that involved people from the United States and outside of the United States. Many issues had been raised, many risks had been identified, and criticality of the project was high. The "how" I did it? Well, I focused on cross-cultural intelligence of myself and each of the team members. And guess what? Yes, I made sure that it was documented in my performance reviews—all of it, and also that my manager's comments were confirming this accomplishment. This is just one of many examples. That is why, if truly needed, not only could I print out and take my performance reviews to my future employer, but they would also contain my manager's comments. This, indirectly, provides reference, recommendations, and endorsements.

From the creation and execution of your executable IDP, the performance reviews are great input. They should be analyzed for your inputs and manager's comments, which would then give you pretty good idea whether your view of yourself is the same view that others see. Of course, first of all, your performance reviews must be solid and written with focus on quality, and if so not done before, make sure they do (start) now.

---

## BONUS TIP:

Your Performance Reviews are your internal resume—and they also complement your external resume.

Be as diligent with Performance Reviews as you are with your resume.

---

Here are five most common questions the professionals that I worked with tended to ask me:

1. How far back I should go to review my past performance reviews? *The rule of thumb is three years. If your performance reviews had been conducted once a year, then this is the very minimum, yet if your performance reviews have been conducted more frequently (for example, quarterly) then two years may be enough.*

2. What if I changed companies or managers during this period of time? *It is perfectly okay. I understand that some biases and lack of consistency may be present, yet since you are dealing with qualifiable data, I believe that these*

*changes would be just fine. Truth be told, they are expected to happen.*

3. Should I consider performance reviews conducted with the managers that do/did not like me? *Yes. There is more to "like me" or "do not like me," and it is a topic that we can discuss or you can discuss with your mentor and coach. You have to separate that from the performance review and accept the content as is. So, yes, it should be considered.*

4. My past performance reviews were superficial, from my and my manager's standpoint. We did them just because the Human Resources department told us that we had to. What should I do now? *First of all, I hope you just learned a lesson, which is to treat your performance reviews seriously. It may be hard at the beginning as this requires a paradigm shift and potential culture change, yet the value and benefit of doing them right, with utmost quality, is imperative. With that said, I would encourage you to disregard previous performance reviews, yet at the same time start with/use the very next one.*

5. I work for a small company and we do not have formal performance reviews. I never had one. What should I do? *Given the employment laws, in order to maintain records of performance, from hiring to firing, there ought to be a process of employee performance reviews. With that said, if indeed there is not one, I would encourage you to do these three things: one is to maximize the use of the 360 degree feedback tool (explained earlier in the book); the next one is to self-initiate periodic (preferably quarterly) performance reviews with your manager—focusing on both, the "whats" you are doing and "hows" you are doing, and last one*

*is to update and analyze your resumé (more about analyzing a resumé in the next section).*

There are many more questions that I get asked pertaining to performance reviews, merely because professionals think of performance reviews seriously for the first time when they read this book or hear my talk.

After you gather your past performance reviews, the analysis should start. You should analyze them for the following items:

- Where your inputs and comments are consistent with your manager's
- Where your inputs and comments are different from those of your manager's
- Where your and your manager's inputs complement each other's
- Are there trends in any comments; are there comments that repeat either within the same performance review or across multiple performance reviews (over time)
- Reflect on your accomplishments and how you felt about working on those things that led to the accomplishment
- Anything that may be stated only once in any of the performance reviews that you either feel or know that it was unique (and why was it unique— why never happened again)
- Anything else that you think would be of benefit as you continue to work on your executable IDP

Note that my experience and experiences of a few others tells me that doing the analysis alone leads to better results and better inputs into your executable IDP. The primary reason for doing it alone is to prevent any noise and bias being introduced into the analysis.

Consistently with the previous steps, the outcomes of this step shall be inserted into your "Personal Profile Matrix."

## External Assessment: Plus Specific One

Similarly to the previous step where you were finding out who you are (the internal view), this step, finding where you stand (the external view), would be incomplete without an assessment or feedback related directly to your chosen career path. Depending which career path, SME, PRM, or PPL, you chose, I would highly suggest that you research and find one more specific-to-your-career-path method of finding where you stand. Alternatively to finding a specific method to generate additional feedback would be to complete a detailed analysis of your complete resumé. This would only be a good idea, if and only if, you plan to continue to serve in the same industry—and maybe even the same employer.

Selma, is an SME. She initially struggled to find a balance between what was expected of her and what she was actually good at. As she was going through the process of creating her executable IDP instead of having to find additional methods of collecting feedback and finding where she stood, she decided to analyze her resumé. She was the first person that did it, and since it worked for her, it is now included as an alternative in this process.

Analyzing one's own resumé requires a process to be followed. It requires balance between discipline and reflection as well as objectivity and subjectivity.

Your first step is to make sure your resumé is complete and up to date. This is not a time to make it pretty or condensed or to omit any work, education, skills, volunteering experiences, or anything else for that matter. Once you have your resumé full and completely up to date, then you need to go through it, preferably with two highlighters of different colors. First, highlight everything that you have done or learned and were energized by. Usually, those things are fun to remember and still energize you—maybe even put a smile on your face. Then you need to do the same, except this time, highlight everything that you have done or learned, yet you would rather never do again. You can recognize these things pretty easily since most of them would be things you tried to forget. Once you are finished, your resumé will have a brand new character to it. The next step is to analyze your accomplishments. This is a pretty straightforward task, as all you need is to differentiate between those accomplishments reached by working on a team versus those accomplishments reached by working alone. The significance of knowing which is which is vast because the next you would need to do is, again, highlight which of the two were more energizing for you. Working in a team or working alone. Stick with the same colors for easier organization later. Recognitions are next. If you ever been recognized, by either your manager or anyone else inside or outside of the organization, you want to identify and differentiate between those recognitions. Differentiate between where you were recognized as a part of a team and those recognitions where you were recognized for individual work. Repeat the process of highlighting which of the two was more energizing.

The last three steps in analyzing your resumé have to do with your experiences, education, and skills. First, write down or circle all experiences listed on the resumé.

Follow that with writing-in any additional information. Primarily, add some details about the "whats"—what was the experience, as well as the "hows"—how did you experience it. Second, analyze your education, focusing primarily on what did you learn / study and how did you like it? Also, if the education was formal (academic) or informal (training) in nature. The third and last step is to look into the skills. At this step, try to pinpoint skills that are hard-skills or soft-skills, and how often do you see yourself using each of them. As you probably realized by now, analyzing your own resumé requires time, patience, and reflection. It requires discipline, objectivity, and subjectivity. By the time you are finished, you will never look at your or anyone else's resumé the same way again! The outcome of all of this analysis should be input into your "Personal Profile Matrix." By now your "Personal Profile Matrix" should be a sizeable file with a lot of information about you.

---

## BONUS TIP:

Next to your accomplishment, you may want to write duration— how long did it take to reach the accomplishment. This will give you an idea if you prefer to work on quick and shorter assignments or lengthy and demanding assignments.

---

As a side note, an additional benefit of going through this process is that the next version of your resumé will most likely be much better. At the same time, the very next chance you get to review someone else's resumé (friend, co-worker, candidate) you will be able to apply significantly improved critical thinking to it.

To conclude this step, I have to ask you some simple questions: You feel profiled yet? Feel vulnerable? Feel exhausted? All of the above? I bet you do! The great news is that you are done. Almost done. The hard part and the long parts are behind you.

This is also a good time to take a break. I suggest you take a break and then when you come back, revisit your "Personal Profile Matrix." Check to see if you are missing anything or if additional clarification is needed, or if you think you need help before moving to the next step. You can always reach out to my team and I, and we would be happy to help you. Also, if you are creating your executable IDP in parallel with one of your friends, peers, co-workers, or even your manager or mentor, this would also be a good time to ensure together you are still making progress and that you both have reached this point.

Before you move onto the next step and start acknowledging and mapping out any and all gaps between where you are today and where you want to be in the future, I would like to share with you one more quick story. Jonathan is from Vietnam and this is his American name. He graduated with a Bachelor's degree in engineering from an university in Vietnam. He came to the United States to complete his Master's in Business Administration (MBA) as well as to work. "I was hired as an entry level engineer and enrolled at the local public university that had reputable MBA program. In parallel to working on my MBA, I also worked on creating my executable IDP. Two years later, I graduated with an MBA, and at about the same time I completed this process of creating my executable IDP." When I asked him about his experiences of going through the MBA and creating his executable IDP at the same time, his response was, "I was double-dipping!" Later he elaborated to me, "The things I needed to do for this process I was also able to use for school, and vice-versa. For example, the I he was developing through school, I was also able to use for completing the work related to this process." As an author and guy behind the idea of this process, I was more than happy to hear it and even more happy that I was able to help him. Jonathan continues to work on his career and with his drive and executable IDP in place, I am confident he will reach his full potential and achieve his career objectives.

As for you, the next steps will focus on the actual, physical, creation of your executable IDP.

# TIPS FOR YOUR 1:1 WITH MANAGER

## Before the Meeting
- ☐ Read the Step 6 in Section II
- ☐ Schedule the meeting
  - o Invite: Your direct supervisor / manager only
  - o Subject: "Discuss Individual Development Plan: Step 6 - COMPLETED"
  - o Objective: To share with your manager your learnings in the Step 6 your research results about the External View as well as to discuss the next step (Step 7)

*Recommendation: Schedule the meeting at least one week in advance*

## During the Meeting
- ☐ Share with your manager your learnings in the Step 6, and your findings about the External View and share your "Personal Profile Matrix"
- ☐ Seek feedback and any examples where he/she may have observed you that matches or differentiates from the External view results
- ☐ Ask your manager with whom else should you share your results

*Recommendation: Encourage your manager to read and complete Step 6 and share the findings with you and the team*

## After the Meeting
- ☐ Send summary of the meeting
  - o Remind the manager about the next step (Step 7) + express your appreciation (Thank You)

**Write Your Meeting Notes Here:** _____

_____

_____

# How to: **Identify and acknowledge the gaps**

*This chapter provides explanation, examples, tips, suggestions, and tools that will help you successfully complete the step seven, "Step 7: Identify and acknowledge the gaps"*

T he fact that you are reading this chapter means that you either completed all the steps before or are just curious what the step seven consists of. Well, if you have completed all the steps before, then "Congratulations!" You made it beyond the research part of creating your executable IDP. So far so good! Now, it is time to move into actionable steps, and steps that produce a physical, concrete, executable IDP. The prerequisite for this step to be completed is that you have to first set your mindset right—to accept that there is a gap. Perhaps, there are many gaps. Only then can you start by identifying those gaps and acknowledging those gaps, also known as performing the gap analysis.

To begin, you need full engagement of the left hemispheres of your brain: the left side controls logic—and more specifically, you need the full engagement of the part of your brain called "prefrontal cortex." The prefrontal cortex will help you with planning, attention,

---

and decision-making. Do not worry, this step is not rocket science—or brain science—yet it is a step that requires making connections and looking into those connections for any gaps. Ideally, you will make the connections the way your brain makes connections—using dendrites and axons. They make sure that neurons make synaptic connections to other neurons, ultimately resulting in a functional, supernatural brain that can function and reach its full potential. Just like you will be able to reach your full potential and achieve your career objectives.

---

## BONUS TIP:

Believing that there are no gaps means that you either reached your full potential or you set your success level too low. In either case, you need to go back to the beginning of this process and repeat it. But next time with a help of a professional coach from our team.

---

By definition, from the business dictionaries, performing gap analysis incorporates a technique that determines what steps need to be taken in order to move you from your current state to your desired future state. It also means, based on the management literature, the comparison of your actual state with your full potential state. Lastly, from the pure process and projects standpoint, performing gap analysis is determining what you need to do to meet your individual professional (career) objectives. All of these definitions are applicable here, yet furthermore, as you go through this step, you will be able to recognize them and benefit from them. This is one of the fun steps and, as you will see, it is also one of the most beneficial steps in this process. The outcome of this step will generate the actions that will be entered into your physical executable IDP. It will generate a great deal of conversation and planning with your manager, your mentor and coach, as well as your friends and network in general. As a bonus, this step usually generates new energy and self-motivation, both needed during the execution of your executable IDP. Most importantly, the outcome of this step is exactly what you need to address, the gap that you need to close, in order to be successful, to reach your full potential and achieve your career objectives.

A client of mine, called Brad (his actual name and used with his permission), whom I met at one of my speaking engagements, had been searching for ways to advance his career. "I have been disappointed for a long time—with the status quo, and the lack of investment in my by my manager. So, I signed up for as many trainings, seminars, public talks and networking events as I could physically—and mentally—attend." Hence, that is how we met. He was getting tired, over-informed, and sadly still did not see any benefits or progress. A few weeks after we met, we connected in person for lunch and started discussing his disappointments and steps he was taking to overcome them. Before the food was even served it was apparent to me that Brad was lost. He was all over the place and truly did not know what to work on—what gaps existed that he needed to close. Before the lunch was over, he made two commitments to himself (and me); first, that he would stop aimlessly going after every training, seminar, talk, and networking event that he could find; and second, "I will make 'gap analysis' my primary and only task." Brad, different from many other clients, started with this step instead of the step one. Eventually, he did complete the entire process from the beginning to the end. The results of us working together, and him following this process, resulted in him referring many clients to me. Yet for him, he became a director at a different company, and still today attends trainings, seminars, talks, and networking events, yet only those that continue to close the gaps between his future state and current state. He has far more time, and he is far more intentional and effective. Since we started working together, Brad also got married, had his first child, and relocated to a different city. Brad, when you read this, please say hi to Brad junior and your lovely wife and thank you for trusting me and this process with your career.

With Brad's story and experience behind us, it is time that you get your "Personal Profile Matrix" and your "Research Results Matrix" out in the open. If you have them both electronically saved, this would be a good time to either have two monitors, one matrix per monitor, or maybe even print them both out and tape them to the wall of your room or office. At the time of writing this step, I am actively helping nine different people to create their own executable IDPs. Six of these nine are well into the process; one is nearly finished, while two are just starting. As you can imagine, I am working with electronic files only, since there is not enough wall-room for all these matrixes to be displayed at the same time! When you are selecting the place to work, keep in mind that this step can take quite bit of time, and that you need uninterrupted blocks of time. Your living room or cubicle, for example, would be a bad choice while your office or spare bedroom at home, for example, would be an excellent choice. Once you have both matrices readily available and displayed, you can begin the work.

To ensure that you identify all the gaps between your current state and your future state—considering all of the data and information gathered, you should break it down into four stages. The first stage should be limited to identifying gaps related to your education. This stage is quickest and easiest, and hence would create a quick win and generate the initial momentum. The second, and a bit more demanding stage focuses on identifying gaps related to your skills. In the next stage, and ultimately the most demanding, you will identify gaps related to your experiences. The last stage is most general and catchall stage. In this stage, you will identify all other gaps that may exist. This stage is covered in greater detail at the end of this chapter.

**First Stage: Gaps Related to Education**

When it comes to identifying gaps in your education, to be true to yourself and those in your network, it is important to consider only *completed* education. In other words, if you are currently enrolled in a degree-seeking program or going through a developmental training through your employer, such education should not be considered completed. As Aesop, the Greek fable writer who lived around 620 to 560 BC in his fable "The Milkmaid and Her Pail," wrote *"Do not count your chickens before they are hatched."* If, indeed, you would count education in progress as completed, you would cheat yourself from number of different angles. Primarily, from a time and timing perspective, to fully understand what your first steps in the execution of your executable IDP should be. On the other hand, by being brutally honest and detailed, you will have a true reality check and a more fruitful conversation with your mentors and managers. Just to illustrate this point, I will share with you a story of my brother. My brother has been recognized as very talented in his profession and as such has been growing his career in a steady progressive pace. In fact, for last five years, he has moved up the chain twice and almost doubled his salary. His network, even though it could use some more work, has been solid, and his current company and boss appreciates his performance. The lesson he learned in a hard way is related to his attempt to expand his responsibilities. While working on his master's degree, which he completed at the top of the class, he applied for a position that would give him increased responsibilities— so called, "job enlargement." This was something on which he would enjoy working. He followed all of the proper steps, from researching the position, to connecting with his network, to applying for the position and preparing for the interviews. Throughout the process, he had been encouraged to keep proceeding and with "all ducks in a row," he thought the position was his. Well, one of the ducks was off, and that was his master's degree. The position required successful completion of master's level studies, from which he was one semester. Even though he received a lot of positive feedback from the hiring manager and recruiter, he was not selected for the position he applied for. Reason: failed to meet basic qualifications. To say that he was disappointed would be an understatement. Beyond him, his network was disappointed too. As of writing of this book, he is working on repairing his network and working on his rebound. Hard lesson to learn, yet completely avoidable.

## BONUS TIP:

You can further evaluate the differences between your education (and school, curriculum, etc.) with the education of the successful people by referring to publications that describe and rank schools and programs.

By completing this stage properly and making sure that you identify all of the gaps related to education, your executable IDP can be as solid as it should be. With that said, to complete this stage in your "Personal Profile Matrix," look for the section where you have documented your current education. Make sure you recall all your notes, including those generated by talking with your mentors and managers. Next, go into your "Research Results Matrix," and locate the results of your research related to education obtained by those you deemed successful. Ideally, you may want to pull those two sets of information: information about your current education in "Personal Profile Matrix," and information about the education of successful people in "Research Results Matrix," together and place them side by side. Once you have this done, the rest is easy.

Simply compare the two sets of information, from the following set of criteria:

- Level of education: high school, associate degree, bachelor's degree, master's degree, doctorate, post-doctorate, and anything in between
- Type of education: engineering, business, economic, social, sciences, etc.
- School category: community college, academic university, research university, military school, or any other
- Beyond academics: look for professional development and education received from seminars, special training, one-off courses and classes as well as instructions received for a specific job, assignment and so on

There may be additional criteria that you may want to consider, things like school rankings, program curriculums, internships, and other relevant criteria.

Once you have all the educational gaps identified and acknowledged, write the gaps, in some level of detail, into a new document—which I call: "My Executable IDP." For your convenience, I have included a sample template for creating "My Executable IDP" on the book's website. Before moving to the next stage, you should go over—at least one more time—the two matrices to make sure you covered everything, to ensure that all the gaps have been accounted for and documented in your "My Executable IDP." Only then you can move to the next stage, which is identifying the gaps in your skills.

**Second Stage: Gaps Related to Skills**

Acknowledging and identifying the skills gap is a significantly harder and longer task than doing the same for the educational gaps. It is because people, perhaps including yourself, always think that their skills are much better, more advanced, and more proficient than they truly are. This stage usually requires additional conversations with a coach, preferably a professional coach, or at least a mentor and manager. As I mentioned before, I am currently working with nine different individuals, coaching them to develop their own executable IDPs and one of them just completed this stage. It took every bit of ninety days to do it, and it was because he initially had a hard time acknowledging the gaps as they were. He asked me not to use his real name, so we agreed that I would refer to him as "Mr. iHAS" (Mister I Have All Skills). Mr. iHAS is a manufacturing engineer by trade and currently works as Global Program Engineering Manager. Due to his age and current family situation, he is also working on transitioning from corporate America to a private consulting business. When we first met, and started talking about creating his executable IDP, I was a bit puzzled that he would want one. The truth is, Mr. iHAS is the oldest person I have ever coached. Also, I have learned from him about his practical approach to everything, which is just as much, or more, benefit to me as he has learned from me. The same was the case with identifying and acknowledging the gaps in his skills. The initial self-assessment of identifying and acknowledging his skills resulted in no gaps. None! Not a single one. And this assessment was done between Mr. iHAS current skills and skills of some world-renowned experts and consultants. After he completed the self-assessment and I had a chance to look it over, I knew that a long and tough conversation lay ahead of us. The following week, after reviewing the self-assessment, instead of having a telephone conversation, we managed to meet in person. We discussed the skills of the people he deemed successful and aspired to become. Surprisingly, we agreed on just about everything. Yet, when we started discussing Mr. iHAS' skills, we differed—on just about everything. This is where Mr. iHAS' practical approach came to light again. He proposed that we create a list of all skills that we disagreed about and then go through an assessment of each, grading the outcome of the assessment as either "equivalent" or "insufficient"—relative to the same level of the skills of those successful people. This was new to me, but I was willing to try. This was also time-consuming on my, and his, part, yet we were both committed. Finally, since this was his idea, he agreed that no matter what the ultimate results of the analysis were, he would trust the process and acknowledge the gaps. Fast-forward nine days; we had exhausted the checklist. He completed over ten unique skills assessments. Note: after the initial conversation, we went back and identified only the critical skills on which we wanted to complete the assessments, while for other skills we met somewhere in a middle-ground. Once all assessments were completed, we had all skill-gaps identified and acknowledged. Since we used the checklist, we pretty much copied-and-pasted the outcome of the checklist into Mr. iHAS' "My Executable IDP."

---

## BONUS TIP:

When in doubt, check it out! If need confirmation of your skill, have a (professional) coach evaluate it with you. This way, you can be sure that your input into your EIDP is solid.

---

You may choose to create and use a checklist to complete this stage. It may help you identify and acknowledge the gaps, yet you may also proceed without the checklist. Without the checklist, you need to repeat the similar process as in previous stage. Use your "Personal Profile Matrix" and segregate your own skills, including the level of proficiency, as well as using your "Research Results Matrix" and again segregate the skills (including the proficiency) of those people you selected. Again, from my experience working with number of clients and direct reports in the past, I would suggest placing those sets of skills next to each other—either on the wall or two separate computer screens, and comparing them line by line, skill by skill.

Here are some watch-outs and tips you can use to perform this task:

- Where you have objective evidence (i.e. resumé, references, personal experience) of the skill and level of proficiency of the successful person that you are doing the gap analysis against, compare those skills first

- When you are uncertain of the particular skill level of the successful person, assume the proficiency level of an expert
- Compare and perform a gap analysis of hard skills first. According to the Investopedia, as well as mentioned on the "Business Skills" website, these skills are such that are specific, teachable, can be defined and measured. Hard skills include skills such as typing, writing, math, reading, the ability to use certain software programs, fluency in a foreign language and programming
- Do not forget or take too lightly to perform a gap analysis of the soft skills. They may be soft skills, yet they are hard to evaluate. With Mr. iHAS we needed to use special sessions and methods of gathering additional feedback in order to properly assess his soft skills—this was both time consuming and costly. Remember, by contrast to hard skills, soft skills are less tangible and harder to quantify. They include such skills as etiquette, getting along with others, listening, engaging in small talk, adaptability, and problem-solving
- In case you have never done skill-assessments or gap analysis related to your skills and skill levels, there are a number of ways to learn to do it—and most of it is free and available online or by picking up a book at your local bookstore

Understanding that a skills gap analysis can be a taxing task for many professionals, I also suggest hiring a coach or ask your mentor or manager for assistance. In case of Mr. iHAS, he had asked me, but you can choose to ask anyone you trust and deem competent to help.

Once you have completed the skills analysis by identifying and acknowledging all of the gaps in skills and skills levels between your current state and of those you deemed successful, update your "My Executable IDP."

**Third Stage: Gaps Related to Experiences**

In the step six, "Step 6: Learn where you stand—External View," I introduced you to Tah, an individual contributor that started his career in a small commodity business, which was later acquired by a large international company. Recall, or even better, revisit, his story above, of him being a high contributor while gaining vast experiences wearing multiple hats. Later he was seen as a low contributor that lacked being a team player. He is a typical example of where early experiences and reputation can, over time, significantly deteriorate. This can happen either because of things under your control or things outside of your control. Because of that, it is important that you compare your overall experiences, which should include good and bad, yet at the same time primarily focus on your most current experiences—again, good and bad. Just like Tah, many professionals have a tendency to exaggerate their experiences. With that, they convince themselves that their experiences are greater than they actually are. This was certainly one of the major deal-breakers between Tah and I, and the reason we decided not to work together on creating his executable IDP.

You and I both understand that the successful people you have selected most probably have had a different path. They also dealt with different circumstances throughout their careers. They had to make different decisions, were surrounded by different people than those that you may ever be. Still, your analysis should be about identifying and acknowledging the gaps in: thought-through thinking, approach to dealing with people, handling different circumstances (aka situational leadership), making decisions, as well as the scope of the work which you should master. It sounds complicated, yet it is really not. Here is why. For example, if one of your selected people is Omar Ishrak, Bangladesh-born Chairman and Chief Executive Officer of Medtronic who transformed a traditional medical device company into a leader of Therapy Innovation, Economic Value, and Global Presence, and with that expanded patient access to healthcare around the world. In both of these cases, the chances of you being in a position and time to experience exactly the same experiences they have had, are none. At the same time, the type of experiences, such as experiencing cost cutting measures, making tough decisions about people and products, transforming small or midsize or large business, and simply experiencing diversity and adversity similar to them is very probable. With that said, there is nothing wrong in aspiring to become next Omar Ishrak, yet your focus should be on identifying and acknowledging the gaps in experiences that they have versus those you have.

To bring you back down to earth and to make this step more relevant, let me tell you one concrete example. Supposedly, your selected successful person has indeed made some significant contributions in your industry. And one of the ways he or she has achieved that is through being able to make very tough decisions and trade-offs on what kind of projects his or her organization would work. These decisions are always hard to make as they impact peoples' lives, morale of the employees, company current and future financial stability, as well as brand, reputation and operational culture. You, on the other hand, have not had a chance to experience the same. You can identify and acknowledge this as a gap and put it into your "My Executable IDP." Chances of you—as you continue to develop towards your full potential and reaching your career objectives—experiencing the same tough decisions is there for you to grab. Furthermore, if you have selected SME as your career path, then identifying and acknowledging gaps in your experiences pertaining to things such as investigative research, value-added teaching, and effective public speaking is very much relevant and important.

For me, it is hard to be any more specific without working with you one-on-one in developing your specific executable IDP, yet I believe you got the message and the examples are helpful. Again, this stage, of the four stages included in this step, is the hardest and longest to complete. Yes, it will also be the hardest and longest to close—from the gap standpoint. However, once you have all the gaps identified and acknowledged them, it is time to include them into your "My Executable IDP."

With the three stages down, you have only one more to go, the stage that deals with identifying and acknowledging the gaps related to "everything else."

**Forth Stage: Gaps Related to Everything Else**

The first three stages focused on the core competencies and core requirements of any career. The fourth, and the last stage, focuses on "everything else"—everything else that is relevant to your chosen career path and your career objectives. In this stage, you need to identify and acknowledge any and all gaps related to things listed below.

Note that this list, even though extensive and research-based, is by no means universal or presented in any particular order:

- Business acumen: How they obtained and demonstrated the business acumen at different levels and different stages of their career
- Professional certifications: Which of the professional certifications made the most significance and contributions towards reaching their success
- Extracurricular activities: What extracurricular activities they benefited from, and what influenced them to participate in them
- Professional exposures: This may be tricky to identify. The common misconception is that you have to have a high-level title in order to report to a high-level person in the organization, or that you have to have a high-level title in order to be responsible for strategic initiatives. In reality, there are many examples where a project manager, without any direct reports, reports to the head of the organization and indeed works on some high confidential, business crucial, strategic initiatives
- Extra projects: Projects that were, at one point or another, performance stretch goals, or perhaps specific projects that shaped their careers—either in a positive or negative light as well as what lessons they learned from them
- Volunteer experiences: Especially with non-profit organizations and professional associations where they had a chance to directly add-value
- Internships: Depending where you are in your career, internships provide an opportunity to launch your career and development like a rocket into space

- Religious work: It is not required to be religious or follow the same faith as the people you have selected as successful, yet it is important to understand how their worldview has been influenced and shaped by their religious beliefs as well as how that impacted their development, and perhaps any charitable or missionary works
- Social activities: Engaging in peer-based events such as playing golf, or participating in parent-teacher associations, or frequent entertainment of family and friends
- Personal values: What values are not negotiable and with that not compromised. How they found out what those values are for them
- Support network: How they built their Personal Board of Directors or how they went about building their teams at work
- Leadership / Communication styles: What is their natural leadership and communication style versus which style they have to exhibit in the public? Also, how they learned to manage between the two, especially if/when there is a conflict between them
- Inclusion and Engagement: Their ability to include people from different backgrounds and engage them into solving common problems by applying unique perspective
- Passion / Drive / Motivational factors: What drives them to win, to succeed, and how that changed over the course of their career and their professional development
- Emotional Intelligence: In particular, how people perceived them. For example, if they are perceived as helpful and willing to invest in others or self-promoter with personal agenda at all times

It is okay if, during your research, you have found some of the information above but not all of the information, as long as you cover each of the bullet points at least once. If you failed to cover each point at least once, you may need to take a break and revisit the step three, "Step 3: Perform the research."

At this time, you may realize that the road ahead of you is getting paved. At least the foundation has been laid and boundaries have been established. It is becoming more clear, and more understood, which direction you will be going and how you will get there. The excitement and energy should be rising, and with that the motivation to turn your dreams into your goals. It is normal. It is expected. And it is needed. The challenge ahead of you is how to best keep the balance between excitement and patience. Excitement due to having a pretty good idea what to work on and patience to follow the process all the way through—and ultimately, execute your executable IDP.

# TIPS FOR YOUR 1:1 WITH MANAGER

**Before the Meeting**
- ☐ Read the Step 7 in Section II
- ☐ Schedule the meeting
  - o Invite: Your direct supervisor / manager only
  - o Subject: "Discuss Individual Development Plan: Step 7 - COMPLETED"
  - o Objective: To share with your manager your learnings in the Step 7 and inform your manager about the gaps you have identified and acknowledged as well as to discuss the next step (Step 8)

*Recommendation: Schedule the meeting at least one week in advance*

**During the Meeting**
- ☐ Share with your manager your learnings in the Step 7, and inform him/her about the gaps and how you went about identifying them
- ☐ Seek manager's support, means, and ways which would help you start closing the identified gaps
- ☐ Ask your manager what you can do to start and expedite closing of the gaps that you have identified and acknowledged in this step

*Recommendation: Encourage your manager to read and complete this step and share the results with you and the team*

**After the Meeting**
- ☐ Send summary of the meeting
  - o Remind the manager about the next step (Step 8) + express your appreciation (Thank You)

**Write Your Meeting Notes Here:** _____
_____
_____
_____
_____

# How to: **Write down and commit to your EIDP**

*This chapter provides explanation, examples, tips, suggestions, and tools that will help you successfully complete the step eight, "Step 8: Write down and commit to your EIDP."*

Notice that the title of this step is "Write down and commit to your EIDP." Before anything, there is emphasis on first *writing down*, and ultimately *committing to* your executable IDP. This could have easily been titled as "Write down!" and "Commit to!" to your IDP, and it would more correctly illustrate and demonstrate the directive and importance of this step.

---

**BONUS TIP:**

Wise person once said, "if you do not document, it will not happen"

---

Norma Reid, a certified executive coach and trainer as well as the owner of "From Dreams to Reality Success

---

Coaching and Training," wrote that professionals that write down their goals and plans have an over 80% higher chance of realizing the same goals. This is in comparison to those who do not write down theirs. In addition to that, there have been numerous studies and research done showing the correlation between writing your goals, objectives, and plans versus achieving them. Universities such as Tulane University from New Orleans, Louisiana; Northern Illinois University from DeKalb, Illinois; Cheyney University from Cheyney, Pennsylvania; University of Kansas, from Lawrence, Kansas; and University of Massachusetts from Dartmouth, Massachusetts are only a few among many more institutions that have researched, and published work related to writing down goals, objectives, and plans in order to increase your chances of achieving them. In fact, one of those studies was done by Forbes magazine. Forbes reported a remarkable study about goal-setting carried out in the Harvard Master's in Business Administration (a.k.a. MBA) Program. In this study, only 3% of the students had written goals and plans to accomplish them, 13% had goals in their minds but had not written them down, and 84% had no goals at all. Ten years later, the same group of students was interviewed again, and the conclusion of the study was totally astonishing. The 13% of the class who had goals, but did not write them down, earned twice the amount of the 84% that had no goals. At the same time, the 3% who had written goals were earning, on average, ten times as much as the other 97% of the class combined.

In addition to the earnings—financial benefits—here are seven added reasons that research shows why you should write down your plans, objectives, and goals:

1. Keeps the most important thing being the most important thing

2. Eliminates distractions and minimizes detours
3. Frees up room in your mind to take your thinking to the next level (frees up your personal RAM)
4. Becomes tangible and (easily) shareable with your mentors and managers
5. Remains consistent at all times
6. Creates commitment to self and raises accountability to execution
7. Helps to review, recognize, and celebrate the progress

Now, let's look at the alternative: Not writing down your plan. What happens, or better said, what does not happen when you do not write down your goals? What are the consequences of not writing down your goals? Can you think of any? Remember the last time you made your new year's resolutions come true? What about your "getting back in shape" goal? How is your goal of achieving work-life balance coming along? Why is your healthy nutrition, eating more greens and drinking more water instead of eating fast-food and drinking soda, more like a yo-yo diet instead of steady continuous improvement? Did you write any of these or other failed goals and plans on paper? I think you got the message. Writing down your executable IDP, and then committing to your executable IDP is imperative for increased chances of reaching your full potential and achieving your career objective.

In my attempt to help as many professionals as I can, there has only been one instance where I worked with the same individual twice. Her name was Angelica. The reason Angelica and I needed to work together again was simply due to her skipping this step. By not writing down her plan, not only that she failed to execute it and make progress towards her full potential, but she mostly forgot what her plan was in the first place. She even misplaced the gap analysis, which, for the most part, you do not need once you have your plan in place. Needless to say, Angelica and I were both a bit frustrated, yet we worked together to re-build and finish creating her executable IDP. I am happy to report that, today, Angelica has a written plan in place and a pocket-version (more about pocket version and other versions of the plan later in this step) too, readily available, and proudly shares it with her network.

---

**BONUS TIP:**

For templates, help and to contact me and members of my team, go to this book's website.

---

I admit that it is tempting to just move into the execution, to start focusing on closing the gaps instead of "wasting" any time on writing down those gaps. It requires patience to cross the finish line, yet it is an absolute requirement to be able to commit to your plan. To make it easier for you, I have included sample executable IDP templates FREE to download on the book's website. There are multiple versions and you can find them by visiting www.myeidp.com or www.jasminnuhic.com. Now, whether you use the templates provided or create your own personalized versions, your executable IDP should be no longer than two pages (one sheet, front and back). This is the maximum! Making it any longer, it becomes discouraging, as it will appear as a too long of a task list. Instead, it should look like your "resumé of the future"— from the content and structure standpoint. In addition to the resumé-like version of your executable IDP, you may also want to create a pocket-size version. Given the limited real estate on the pocket-size version, you may want to consider creating infographics—visual representations of your executable IDP—by using representative icons, images, pictures, charts, and graphics. Beyond the format, the substance in the content is the key. The content comes directly from your "My Executable IDP." Carefully transcribing the information, taking care of education, skills, experiences, and everything else into the "resumé of the future" is the first action. Take your time to do it wisely and completely.

Finally, as a last action of this step, and overall process of creating your executable IDP, after you have written it down, you should do the following:

- Have your "resumé of the future" printed and displayed somewhere visible
- Share it by sending copies to: your manager, your mentor, coach, and members of your personal board of directors
- If available at work, populate your official Human Resource profile and development plan
- Have one copy, at least the pocket-size version laminated, and with you at all times
- Setup periodic reminders in your phone, Outlook, app, and/or Google calendar, to do progress "health-checks" of your executable IDP
- COMMIT TO your executable IDP

CONGRATULATIONS! You have created your first, or updated and improved, executable IDP! Why wait? Let's put it to use right-away and start to execute it. Go straight to the next step, "Step 9: Execute your EIDP" to find out how.

# TIPS FOR YOUR 1:1 WITH MANAGER

## Before the Meeting
- [ ] Read the Step 8 in Section II
- [ ] Schedule the meeting
  - o Invite: Your direct supervisor / manager only
  - o Subject: "Discuss Individual Development Plan: Step 8 - COMPLETED"
  - o Objective: To share with your manager your learnings in the Step 8 and to share your executable Individual Development Plan as well as to discuss the next step (Step 9)

*Recommendation: Schedule the meeting at least one week in advance*

## During the Meeting
- [ ] Share with your manager your learnings in the Step 8, and your created executable Individual Development Plan (leave one copy with your manager)
- [ ] Seek feedback on your executable Individual Development Plan
- [ ] Ask your manager to continue to loop for opportunities that are aligned with your executable Individual Development Plan

*Recommendation: Be as explicit as possible about your executable Individual Development Plan*

## After the Meeting
- [ ] Send summary of the meeting
  - o Remind the manager about the next step (Step 9) + express your appreciation (Thank You)

## Write Your Meeting Notes Here: _____
_____
_____
_____
_____

# How to: **Execute your EIDP**

*This chapter provides explanation, examples, tips, suggestions, and tools that will help you successfully complete the step nine, "Step 9: Execute your EIDP."*

Whether you have development plan in place or created your executable IDP following the process described in this book, in this chapter you will learn how to execute your plan. It is the only way to reach your full potential and achieve your career objectives.

There are many ways to get from point A to point B. You can choose to walk, skate, ride a bike, go by a car or ship, or you can fly. What you cannot choose is the time you have available to make that journey. The time is the limiting factor. To get the most out of your time, you must break down your plan into manageable chunks. This will prevent you from taking wrong turns and will let you know that you are making progress. Once the breakdown of the plan is in place, you should make a first step, a step that would take you from point A towards point B. To make it more vivid, let's take a flight in an airplane. A pilot, either that be a commercial high-experienced pilot or a private pilot that is new to flying, is required to create and file a flight plan before starting the engine. This flight plan considers the weight of the plane: total load, which may include airplane itself, passengers, cargo, and fuel, the route to be flown, weather throughout the entire flight path, wind, any potential obstacles, communication channels, locations of selected beacons, and additional essentials that are particular for each flight. On top of that, the pilot ensures and checks for airplane's airworthiness, current registrations, and availability of the operating manuals. Finally, the pilot inspects the frame of the airplane and confirms that he or she has everything in place to start the flight. As you noticed, quite a bit goes into the pre-flight planning of each flight. No wonder air transportation continues to be the safest means of transportation in the world. Makes you wonder why we do not do the same when we travel by car, as it may reduce number of accidents and fatalities that are happening every single day. But all this planning that the pilot does has limited to no value unless she or he starts the engines and actually completes the flight. In this case, executes the plan. Only then, when we arrive at point B, do we see the value of the plan we created. The same is true for your executable IDP. Up to this point you have been working hard, spending a lot of time creating your executable Individual Development Plan, and now it is time to execute it, to get value out of it.

---

## BONUS TIP:

A plan without execution is a documented dream that never becomes reality.

---

Just like the pilot, as you were gathering the information and creating your executable IDP, you relied on many people. They included your colleagues, mentors, managers, friends, and family members. Some of these people you will continue to rely on, in some cases much more, while in some cases significantly less. As a professional you should not be looking for teachers or trainers that give you answers to questions you may never encounter. Instead, you need mentors, coaches, and a personal board of directors that help you find the answers at the time you need them. As promised in previous chapters, I will now go into more elaboration about which are the people you will rely on most, and how to make sure that you either have them or get them. For example, I am going to cover the role of the mentor, and how to secure one. If you already have one, that is much better.

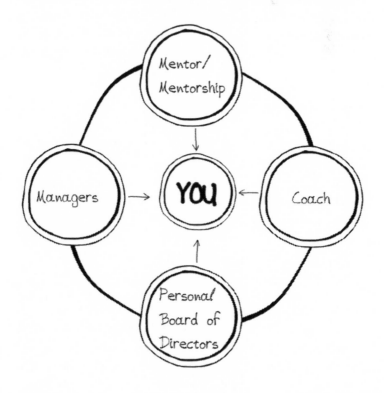

Besides, I am going to cover types of mentorships, and the relationship with a mentor. Similarly, I am going to further introduce you to the concept of "personal board of directors." Lastly, you will find out how your manager fits into all this. These roles, mentor, personal board of directors, and managers are your equivalent of a pilot's traffic controllers, airline weather monitors, and maintenance technicians. Together, they all work in synchronization to ensure as smooth and as safe flight as possible. In your case, positive progress towards reaching your full potential and achieving your career objectives. Afterwards, I am going to clarify the role of a coach and close out this step by sharing with you the importance of breaking down your executable IDP into predefined milestones and ways you can do that. All with the intention of helping you manage the execution with ease and confidence. Lastly, in this step, you will take your first steps in starting the actual execution of your executable IDP. This would be equivalent to the pilot starting the engines.

## Support Role: Mentor

According to Merriam-Webster dictionary, the word "mentor" comes from Greek literature. More specifically, it comes from the epic story of *The Odyssey*, written by Homer. Odysseus had a baby with the name Telemachus that was raised under the supervision of an old and trusted friend named Mentor. Mentor, together with the goddess Athena, educated young Telemachus about his father as well as had a positive, guiding influence on his life. From this came the meaning and concept of "mentor" as a counselor, guide, and trusted advisor. From a professional relationship standpoint, the concept of "mentor" represents a connector and someone with vested interest in the professional development of another, usually younger, person. Furthermore, a mentor is someone who challenges "who or what you are" with "who or what you can be (come)." In today's work, and life environment, a mentor is becoming increasingly important ally to have and a necessary resource to rely on. In this book, if you counted the number of times the word "mentor" is included, you would end up with a count of close to one hundred. It is perhaps one of the most frequent words, and most important roles, that can influence and help you make-or-break the successful execution of your executable IDP.

## Support Role: Mentorship

By definition, mentorship is a relationship between a mentor and a mentee. It is a relationship that is not necessarily exclusive between two people, yet it is a relationship that is based on trust, respect, and confidentiality. It is also a relationship that can be formal or informal as well as gender, race, age, and position independent. A mentorship relationship is, however, strongly desirable that the mentor and mentee share the same profession, work in different reporting structures, and have a strong professional network. In general, mentorship relationships last a lifetime, and the benefits of mentorship relationships are mutual and great. There are many different types of mentorship relationships spreading from peer-to-peer and one-on-one to many-to-one and one-to-many (number of mentors and mentees at any given time). Statistically speaking, the number of mentorship relationships between the late 1970s and 2016 has been growing exponentially. The topic of mentorship has been covered in a great detail by many reputable publications, academic institutions, and professional organizations. One of such publications, and recommended readings, is *The Mentor's Guide: Facilitating Effective Learning Relationships* by Lois J.

Zachary. Lois, in this book, provides examples, worksheets, and templates as well as guides you and your mentor to better outcomes.

**Support Role: Personal Board of Directors**

Personal Board of Directors or PBD is fairly new concept in the world of professional and personal development. It is a concept "shamelessly borrowed" from the publicly traded companies and non-profit organizations. These institutions, in many cases, are required to have a governing body that helps them with direction of their organizations. PBD has been seen as a "value-added" team, and even though it has been required by law since the very early of nineteenth century, it has been in place since before that. Today, even small, privately held, businesses tend to have a board of directors. Inherently, since PBD has been seen as value-added, many professionals started establishing their own PBD. They are, mostly, informal, and unofficial, yet they operate in the similar fashion as the board of directors of publicly traded companies. They can consist of anywhere between three and nine board members. It is recommended to keep the number either five or seven, where seven is the most recommended.

You, as a professional with an executable IDP, should establish and use your PBD for the following reasons:

- To have someone to hold you accountable on all aspects of your executable IDP
- To have someone help you reach certain milestones that otherwise you would not be able reach on your own
- To have someone to open doors and connect you with people that you can mutually benefit

- To have someone you can ask for advice, or even to vent to, with utmost confidence and confidentiality
- To have someone review and adjust your executable IDP, career objectives, and progress towards reaching your full potential

In some ways, PBD sounds like mentorship, yet it is different. It is different in a sense that you should meet with your PBD less frequently than with your mentors. Your board should comprise of people from different spheres of your life. For instance, you may build your PBD by recruiting someone with experience and seniority in your industry, someone with whom you went to college, a trusted friend from a different part of the country, someone that is actively involved with a local non-profit organization, your mentor, your spouse or significant other, partner, or someone from academic, judicial, finance, or faith-based profession. Nevertheless, members of the board should be exempt from owning any tasks yet be constant a provider of relevant resources. They should also be periodic provider of both appreciative and constructive feedback.

Since PBDs are still a fairly new concept, I recommend, and my team can help, you build one customized for you, for your career objectives and your executable IDP.

**Support Role: Manager**

No matter where you are in the organization, even if you are self-employed or Chief Executive Officer of the most successful business, without exception, you have someone that manages you. They may manage your time, your work, or your skills yet they should never manage your development. That is your job. Throughout this book and the process of creating and executing your executable IDP, you can find tips, suggestions, and ideas on how to and when to manage your manager. It is recommended that you revisit, at least those parts of each step, before each time you meet with your manager. Especially, when you are meeting with your manager to talk about the progress made against the execution of your executable IDP. The only additional point I want to remind you of is to absolutely, clearly, with 100% certainty, identify who *is* or who *are* all of your managers. This can be simple and straightforward task in some organizations (i.e. hierarchy-based) and very complex in others (i.e. matrix-based). Knowing this will help you to ensure that you cover the right topics with the right managers at the right time.

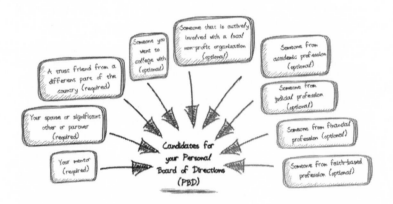

## Support Role: Coach

Last, yet certainly not the least, is a coach. Having a professional coach throughout the entire process of creation and execution of your executable IDP is recommended yet not required. According to *The Coaching Habit: Say Less, Ask More and Change the Way You Lead Forever* by Michael Bungay Stanier, 73% of professionals never receive coaching. And, when they do, the coaching usually does not help them. In fact, fewer than 25% of professionals believe coaching benefited them, and 10% of professionals reported that the coaching, actually, hurt them. My team and I handle numerous coaching engagements at any given time and the experiences have shown us that the role of a coach can help make or break this process, and ultimately your opportunity to reach your full potential and achieve your career objectives. Throughout this book, you can read a number of bonus tips and coaching points, yet due to limited space and specifics that each person requires, not all tips and points are included. As expected, much more is shared during one-on-one sessions and when formal coaching arrangements are made. In the absence of a professional coach, a manager or mentor can step into that role. To get the most out of the process and a coach, I would highly recommend hiring a professional coach. If possible, someone very familiar with this process of creating and executing an executable IDP. Once you do have a coach, you need to make sure that the coach is following you in the same footsteps and in real-time. The coach should not be looking ahead (that is the job of a mentor), should not be going on a side or tangent (that is the job of the members of your PBD), and should not be managing you (that is the job of your manager). Rather the coach should be coaching you in and within the precisely exact step that you are in. It is hard to find a good coach, and it is even harder to keep a good coach unless contractual agreements are made up front. Once you have one, the very first step, together with the coach, should be breaking down your executable IDP into "manageable goals."

Now that you understand different concepts, roles, and responsibilities of mentors, managers, coaches, and personal board of directors as well as different types of mentorship relationships, let's move to the specifics related to the execution of your executable IDP. Lets start with concrete first action, first step, to be taken—and taken immediately.

When it comes to the execution of your executable IDP, you will be following the well-known and documented framework model of professional development. It is known as the "70-20-10" model.

As previously mentioned, the biggest bulk of your time, roughly 70% of your time, you will spend closing the gaps associated with the experiences. Through the experiences, you will be able to learn and make decisions, and work on addressing challenges and opportunities. These will be of different vitality to the organization, will expose you to interactions with influential people, and build your credibility and reputation as well as your personal brand. You will also learn from your mistakes and deal with receiving and giving feedback related to your performance. Some of these experiences, which you need in order to close the experience gap, will come to you yet most of them you should seek out and be intentional about. Make sure you seek them out from within your employer, but also from the outside of your employer, such as non-profit organizations. Note that in this 70%, your interactions with your managers, mentors, and personal board of directors is also included.

The skills are the second most time-demanding area and will account for about twenty-percent of the time to close the skills related gaps. Specific skills that you need to develop are in your "Research Results Matrix," "My Executable IDP," and "Personal Profile Matrix." Beyond the development of your skills in these 20% is also interactions with your coach.

The last, but not least, 10% of your time will be spent closing the gaps pertaining to formal traditional education and training. This may include obtaining a relevant degree and completing appropriate continuous education classes. Depending on your career path and size of the gap between the successful person and your current status, this may be the first area you sign up for and tackle. Even though formal traditional education accounts for only about ten-percent, it can be the single most important thing during the execution of your executable IDP.

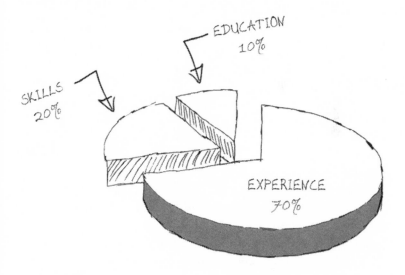

EDUCATION 10%

SKILLS 20%

EXPERIENCE 70%

With the 70-20-10 framework model in mind, it is the time to make a first step, take the first action, and start executing your executable IDP.

At the very beginning of this book and beginning of this process, you learned that your executable IDP shall be title independent, company independent, and time independent. There you also learned of substantial reasons why that should be the case. Now, in the execution step, you are moving from "the whats" to "the whens." With that your executable IDP will start to become time dependent. This is necessary in order to hold yourself, and let others hold you, accountable—and ultimately successful in reaching your full potential and achieving your career objectives. With that said, the first step in executing your executable IDP is to breakdown your plan into "manageable milestones." These milestones should be broken down on short-term, mid-term, and long-term milestones.

---

## BONUS TIP:

70/20/10 learning concept was developed by Morgan McCall, Robert W. Eichinger and Michael M. Lombardo at the Center for Creative Leadership.

---

Depending on your specific case, the definition of each, short-term, mid-term and long-term, milestones will be unique and different. As a guiding principle, the recommendation is to set up short-term milestone in way that can be accomplished no earlier than one year and no longer than two years. The mid-term and long-term milestones to be set between two and five years, as well as five and more years, respectfully. These ranges should be shortened and ultimately milestones made more aggressive for professionals who are later in their career life. Likewise, they could be extended for those professionals that have larger gaps. In any case, some periodic tradeoffs and adjustments will be necessary, and those should be made in conjunction with your work and reviews by your coaches. Take this first step. Go ahead and start the engines and enjoy the process of executing *your* executable IDP as well as reaching your full potential and achieving your career objectives!

# TIPS FOR YOUR 1:1 WITH MANAGER

## Before the Meeting
☐ Read the Step 9 in Section II
☐ Schedule the meeting
  - Invite: Your direct supervisor / manager only
  - Subject: "Discuss Individual Development Plan: Step 9 - COMPLETED"
  - Objective: To share with your manager your learnings in the Step 9 and to provide progress update as well to discuss the next steps

*Recommendation: Schedule the meeting at least one week in advance*

## During the Meeting
☐ Share with your manager your learnings in the Step 9, and progress update, including but not limited to adjustments you are making
☐ Seek feedback on your progress and coaching on how to improve it
☐ Ask your manager to continue to loop for opportunities that are aligned with your executable Individual Development Plan

*Recommendation: Be as explicit as possible about your executable Individual Development Plan*

## After the Meeting
☐ Send summary of the meeting
  - Remind the manager about the next step + express your appreciation (Thank You)

## Write Your Meeting Notes Here: _____
_____
_____
_____
_____

# SECTION III

# The Continuation:
Stick to and Adjust Your EIDP

# Ensuring continuous execution of your EIDP

Professionals that follow this process of creating their executable IDP, by now, usually experience a positive change in their careers. This change is either the result of job enrichment (i.e. promotion within the same company or a new job at a different company) or job enlargement (i.e. increase in responsibility and bigger challenges). Whether this positive change be job enrichment or job enlargement, for only about half of professionals it is a step in the right direction—a step towards fulfilling their full potential and reaching their career objectives. This may be case with you too, in which case it is great news and a great move. For others, which again, may include you, too, it is a distraction from the right track.

Promotion, or a simple job change in any way, is the number one cause of derailment of the execution of your executable IDP. It creates false and temporary career satisfaction that takes your focus away from your long-term career objectives and reaching your full potential. Now, if you are of those lucky ones whose job change has been in direct alignment with execution of their executable IDP, then it is perfectly acceptable to take a deep breath, acknowledge and celebrate the progress. What is more, I would like to congratulate you on the positive progress. On the other hand, if this job change is not directly aligned with your career objectives and does not put you a step closer to reaching your full potential then an immediate adjustment is necessary.

---

## BONUS TIP:

If it is not worth quitting because of it, then it is definitely worth adjusting for it—keep executing your executable Individual Development Plan; No one else *should!*

---

Patience—or better said, lack of patience—is the second most common reason why professionals fail to stick to the execution of their executable IDP. By definition, patience is the state of endurance under difficult circumstances, which includes things such as a delay, physical, or virtual obstacles, and tediousness. It is referred as a character trait and known as "virtue." One of the best ways to overcome the lack of patience is to learn, to develop remarkable willpower, and to increase determination. When it comes to the execution of your executable IDP, patience gets tested each time the execution is stalled, or progress is not being made at the rate of speed that you wanted. Patience also gets tested when other things such as your mentors, managers, coaches, or members of the personal board of directors, change. Patience gets impacted by the circumstances over which you have no control, such as major shifts in economy or industry. Whatever the reason for testing your patience may be, it is imperative to adjust your execution of your executable IDP to fit your patience and external circumstances.

---

The third most common reason why professionals fail to stick with the execution of their executable IDP is the breakdown of planning. As mentioned in the previous step, for a successful execution of your executable IDP, you have to break down your plan into manageable short-term, mid-term, and long-term milestones. This requires discipline that most people do not have as well as requires adjustment as needed to be able to reach them. Of the three most common reasons, this reason is the easiest to correct and adjust to.

The most common reasons why professionals do not stick with the execution of their executable individual Development Plan are:

1. JOB CHANGE
2. PATIENCE
3. PLAN BREAKDOWN

Either that be a temporary distraction because of promotion, or lack of patience, or even inadequate breakdown planning, adjusting the plan and execution is expected—and required. Your plan is like your brain. It is solid and smart, yet it can change as a result of experiences. In this case, because of execution. The change to the plan should be on a micro level, just like the brain changes at the neurons, axons, dendrites, and synapses level. At the same time, your execution is like a flight. To continue from the previous section, once you take off (start with the execution), you must make periodic adjustments due to wind change, turbulence, and requests from the air traffic controllers, all the while keeping your airplane flying towards your ultimate destination—your career objectives and reaching your full potential. As Heraclitus of Ephesus, a Greek philosopher known for his doctrine of change being central to the universe, said *"The only thing that is constant is change,"* and since that is true for the execution of your executable IDP; your coaches, and mentors, together with your managers and members of your personal board of directors, play a critical role in the execution adjustments.

---

## BONUS TIP:

"Four disciplines of execution:
1) Focus on the Wildly Important
2) Act on the Lead Measures
3) Keep a Compelling Scoreboard
4) Create a Cadence of Accountability"

~ Stephen R. Covey

---

To best conclude on how to ensure continuous execution of your executable IDP, please refer to the quote from Colin Luther Powell, an American statesman and a retired four-star general in the United States Army, who was the 65th Secretary of State serving under President George W. Bush. General Powell also served as National Security Advisor and Chairman of the Joint Chiefs of Staff, holding the latter position during the Persian Gulf War. He was the first African American to serve on the Joint Chiefs of Staff. General Powell stated that, *"No battle plan survives contact with the enemy."* This quote, together with the statement that the *"first bullet fired in battlefield requires plan recovery and adjustment,"* best describes that no plan is perfect when it comes to the execution. It is okay, it is needed, it is necessary to make periodic adjustments.

---

Adjustment, either made by a pilot flying a plane, a soldier recovering from the chaos on the battlefield, a project manager leading a project, scientists performing research, or a CEO acquiring a competitor, is better made when inputs from qualified stakeholders are collected and considered. In the case of your execution of your executable IDP, these qualified stakeholders are your coaches, mentors, managers, and members of your personal board of directors. Of course, at any time you need professional help to make proper adjustment and get back on track towards reaching your full potential and achieving career objectives, you can contact anyone from our team. We stand by to help you execute your executable IDP.

# About the Author

Jasmin NUHIC is a passionate author, speaker, facilitator, and coach. He obtained his undergraduate degree in science and holds a master's degree in Business—both from the University of Memphis. He also holds a master's degree in Executive Leadership from Christian Brothers University. Jasmin is certified in Coaching, Ethical Leadership, The OZ Principle, and Cross-Cultural Intelligence. He has global experience in leading and developing individuals and team and is interested in helping others reach their full potential and achieve career objectives.

As a senior partner of "It Starts and Ends with EIDP," Jasmin NUHIC was born and raised in Bosnia and Herzegovina (BiH). In his late teens, and after the war in BiH, together with his mother and younger brother, he moved to the United States of America. Throughout his experiences at the university and later in professional life, he came to realize that *"the best investment is an investment in oneself,"*—meaning education. From that point on, he dedicated his life to teaching at universities and colleges; writing books and articles; public speaking at conferences, seminars, and training, as well as mentoring in the area of professional development.

Today, Jasmin focuses on spreading the message of need for each and every professional to have an executable IDP and with that reach his or her full potential and career objectives.

As an author of this book and subject matter expert in this process, Jasmin would be honored to hear from you— about the impact this book had on you, any grammatical errors, all experiences with this process, and most definitely, any and all success stories. Please feel free to write directly to Jasmin on his email: jasmin.nuhic@myeidp.com.

# Acknowledgement

For this book to become reality, a number of people, organizations, and businesses needed to provide their input, share their experiences, and give support. At this time, I would like to acknowledge, as well as Thank and Recognize these individuals and organizations.

Firstly, I would like to Thank the MY EIDP team for understanding the need for a book such as this one, and giving me a chance to share my research, experiences, and education pertaining to creation and execution of an executable IDP. They provided support through contribution, editing, graphic design, publishing, mentoring, and coaching.

I would like to Thank the companies and individuals that let me share their stories and contributed their materials and references while at the same time they themselves kept looking for new and improved ways to drive people engagement through individual and team development.

Specifically, I would like to Thank my dear friends and critics, as well as contributors, Eric Diep, Sengngeune Vongphrachanh and Nora Akbik Ranjha, as well as Kamaal Anas, Mutlu Celikok, Carolyn White, Garth Conrad, and Michelle Zormeier, for their inputs, feedback, and brainstorming. I would like to also thank Paniz Talesh, a colleague and friend that benefited from this process, and was the first one to create a visual representation of the steps with their respectful inputs and outputs. Her visual representation of the executable IDP has helped many to better understand and benefit from the process.

Last but not least, I would like to Thank the professional organizations and higher-education institutions as well as for-profit businesses that invited me to share this material with their members, students, and employees. This helped with getting real-time feedback, and crystalize the message contained in this book.

And most importantly, I would like to Thank my family, my wife, and kids, for letting me "steal" hours and days at a time from them in order to write and re-write countless number of pages that led into publishing this book. Love ya!

# References and Resources

Since resources and references are an integral part of creating and executing an executable IDP, for your convenience, I have included a number of resources and references that you can take advantage of during creation and execution of your executable IDP. These are the same resources and references I used to develop my own executable IDP as well as what I use when I coach others. Additional resources and references are available on the book's website and through coaching sessions with one of our professional coaching staff.

Declaimer: Some of the resources and references listed below, and on the book's website, require purchase and / or to sign up (share personal information). Neither I nor my organization have ANY interest or gain any benefit from any of them, nor do we serve as mediators between the user and resource / reference.

**Learning Styles Indicator**: assists you in becoming a more effective learner. More information, including videos and links, can be found via "MindTools, Essential Skills for Excellent Career"
*https://www.mindtools.com/mnemlsty.html*

**Career Interest Inventory:** matches your interests with different careers and occupations. Here is reference to Minnesota State career and education resource
*https://www.careerwise.mnscu.edu/careers/clusterSurvey*

**Myers-Briggs Type Indicator® (MBTI®):** helps you identify your primary personality traits, and ultimately provides you with your personality type, which comes from the vast personality inventory
*http://www.myersbriggs.org/my-mbti-personality-type/mbti-basics/*

**Dominance, influence, Steadiness and Conscientiousness (DiSC):** gives you a better understanding of your work style and how to build more effective relationships
*http://www.thediscpersonalitytest.com/*

**StrengthsFinder:** provides you with a personalized Strengths Insight Report, an Action-Planning Guide, and a web-based Strengths Community
*http://strengths.gallup.com/default.aspx*

**Intelligence quotient (IQ):** is a total score derived from one of several standardized tests designed to assess human intelligence. More about the IQ and where you can learn what your IQ is on Wikipedia
*https://en.wikipedia.org/wiki/Intelligence_quotient*

**Emotional intelligence (EI) or emotional quotient (EQ):** is the capability of individuals to recognize their own, and other people's emotions, to discriminate between different feelings, and label them appropriately, to use emotional information to guide thinking and behavior, and to manage and/or adjust emotions to adapt environments or achieve one's goal(s). More about the EQ and how you can assess yours can be found on Wikipedia
*https://en.wikipedia.org/wiki/Emotional_intelligence*

**Five O'Clock Club:** has been applying a proven, targeted, strategic, research-driven approach to career development *https://fiveoclockclub.com/*

**Breaking the Bamboo Ceiling**: Career Strategies for Asians
*http://www.acenet.edu/the-presidency/columns-and-features/Pages/Breaking-the-Bamboo-Ceiling.aspx*

**The Coaching Habit: Say Less, Ask More & Change the Way You Lead Forever**: by Michael Bungay Stanier, from Box of Crayons
*http://www.boxofcrayons.biz/the-coaching-habit-book/*

**The Mentor's Guide: Facilitating Effective Learning Relationships**: by Lois J. Zachary is thoughtful and rich with advice. The Mentor's Guide explores the critical process of mentoring and presents practical tools for facilitating the experience from beginning to end

**Type Dynamics Indicator Form O:** helps you in understanding your personality, preferences and how these relate to your strengths and possible areas for development
*http://www.midasgroup.ie/tdi-type-dynamic-indicator-midas/*

**What the CEO Wants You to Know: How Your Company Really Works**: by Ram Charan, a world-renowned business advisor, author, and speaker.
Ram's YouTube video can be found here: https://www.youtube.com/watch?v=kckNPHodj3g

*All these and other resources, including active links, are available from the book's website:* www.MYeIDP.com.

# About the MY EIDP

*We help individuals, teams, and organizations create and execute their Executable Individual Development Plans through which they can reach their full potential and their career objectives. This inspires us and drives us in our path!*

Think about it, you can spend your dollars on anything from communication skills to management techniques, or you can spend them on developing your employees—your greatest assets. Research shows that over 85% of employees (individual contributors and leaders / managers) to not know how to do it. Our Executable Individual Development Plan coaching, workshops, and keynotes can help you address your need of developing your greatest assets.

## Contact MY EIDP:

**Online:**
www.myeidp.com or www.jasminnuhic.com

**Email:**
contact@myeidp.com

## Connect with the Author Directly:

| | |
|---|---|
| **LinkedIn:**<br>www.linkedin.com/in/jasminnuhic/ | **Twitter:**<br>@Jasmin_NUHIC |
| **Facebook:**<br>www.facebook.com/jasminnuhicauthor | **Email:**<br>Jasmin.NUHIC@myeidp.com |

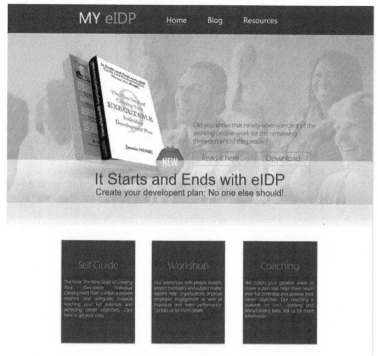

What the readers are saying about the book:

***Think about it***, you can spend your dollars on anything from communication skills to management techniques, or you can spend them developing your employees—your greatest assets.

**Invite us** to speak at your next All Employee Meeting, Conference, or Seminar, as well as to facilitate workshops with your High Potential talent, Conference Attendees, or to provide coaching to individuals and teams.

http://www.myeidp.com

# NOTES: _____

_____

_____

_____

_____

_____

_____

# SCATCHES:

Made in the USA
Monee, IL
17 February 2020

21922075R00102